HOW TO DO LIFE

A Guide To Navigating Life's Challenges and Understanding the World Around You

Giorgio Genaus

www.giorgiogenaus.com

First published in Australia 2021 by Genius Institute

ISBN 978-0-6451969-0-0

Disclaimer

All the information, techniques, skills and concepts contained within this publication are of the nature of general comment only, and are not in any way recommended as individual advice. The intent is to offer a variety of information to provide a wider range of choices now and in the future, recognising that we all have widely diverse circumstances and viewpoints. Should any reader choose to make use of the information herein, this is their decision, and the author and publisher/s do not assume any responsibilities whatsoever under any conditions or circumstances. The author does not take responsibility for the business, financial, personal or other success, results or fulfilment upon the readers' decision to use this information. It is recommended that the reader obtain their own independent advice.

This book is dedicated to you, the reader.

Stay on your quest for answers.

Keep asking your questions and the answers will eventually find you, I promise.

My hope is that you find some answers in these pages.

TABLE OF CONTENTS

"The reading of all good books is like a conversation with the finest minds of past centuries."

RENÉ DESCARTES

PREFACE

When I was a child, I was moved into a bedroom by myself so my sisters could live together in their own room. Because I took up a small amount of room, my bedroom was also used as storage for a mix of things. This included books. There was a dormant fireplace in my bedroom that had the chimney closed off and the firebox painted so my parents fitted a bookshelf in there to store encyclopaedias.

The walls above my bed were lined with hanging bookshelves that were also filled with a wide variety of books. All of these books kept me company whenever I felt lonely and especially if I had woken from a nightmare or panic attack and didn't want to wake my parents. I learnt a lot from these books, but if a book like the one you are reading now had been left somewhere on my bedroom shelves and my parents had told me to open it when I felt troubled, I may have had a very different experience of childhood.

Nonetheless, the way my childhood unfolded was exactly as it was meant to be, which has given me the opportunity to be the author of that book instead of its reader. A reality that is still humbling to this day. I have become the author of the book I wanted to read.

To be clear, I didn't see this book as part of my destiny when I was a child. I anticipated a different life for myself. Life, as it turns out, had anticipated something different for me.

This book came to be as the result of a constellation of experiences making up what was a self-evident picture—an instruction book on navigating life's challenges.

I became aware at a young age that I had navigated an unusual number and variety of challenges, and it was also pointed out to me that the way I thought wasn't like everyone else's way of thinking. That only made me more curious about life and people. So in an attempt to find answers to a growing list of questions about myself and the world, I discovered mentors, authors and fascinating teachings.

As I applied what I learnt in my own life and merged the wisdom and knowledge with my experiences, I came to understand myself and the world very differently. Then one day, while showering, I realised that it'd probably be valuable for me to put these teachings into writing, so I could hand it to someone in the future. I did some research but didn't find an instruction book on life already in existence. If I did, I could've spent the years it took writing this book to do something else. That wasn't my fate, it seems.

I put off starting this book because I had a variety of beliefs telling me I wasn't qualified to write a book of this nature. 'I'm not an expert, influential leader or master of psychology,' I would think.

Until the day came when I was wrestling with my life and I realised that I needed my own words. I needed a book filled with guidance to navigate my challenges. So I selfishly started writing my way through my challenges. As weeks and months passed by and the word count grew, I found myself thinking about you, the reader. I saw you opening up these pages with curiosity and confusion, seeking answers to today's problems.

So I continued to write. I saw this book being held in your hands, ageing with you, getting marks on the cover and pages getting bent as you referred back to it. Then I saw you handing a copy to a dear friend, a child moving out or a loved one and telling them that everything you had learnt about life and yourself you had learnt from applying what you discovered in these pages, much like I did. I saw you saying, "Take this, read this and apply what you read and I know that you're going to be okay." That's all we want for the people we care about, isn't it?

I see this image with confidence because I am the one now handing you this book saying that. I say so, because the contents in this book have ensured that I get to this place in my life today, and that I am who I am because of it.

My mentors of past and present, in death and life, have handed me their pieces of work and said the same to me. Writing this book is me doing the same with you.

Take this book and know that you're going to be okay.

"If I have seen further, it is by standing on the shoulders of giants."

SIR ISAAC NEWTON

INTRODUCTION

One of the hardest things in life can be working out where you are.

Most people focus on where they want to go. They dream up some destination and visualise a promised land of fulfilment, inspiration and contentment. This presents a series of problems.

1. You'll need a map to work out how to get to your destination.

2. You'll have to work out where your destination is on the map.

3. You'll have to work out where you are on the map.

4. You'll have to know how to keep yourself on course.

It's said that life is about the journey and not the destination. What isn't spoken about is the importance of having a compass for the journey.

The truth is that life is filled with roadblocks, obstacles, distractions, drama and confusion along with moments of getting stuck, cornered, burnt out and disheartened. In all my years as a human being and as an advisor to many people, I have found that when we're in the middle of a challenge, we lose our bearings. That is, if we had our bearings in the first place.

This book is like a compass. It doesn't specifically tell you which way to go or what direction you should face. It simply tells you which direction you're facing at any given moment and how you ended up facing that way. The whirlwind of life tends to feel exaggerated when we don't have our bearings. This book helps you find your bearings in the midst of your mind's confusing emotions, lopsided perceptions, distorted memories, wild imagination and insistent repetition. The moment your compass's needle finds north, everything becomes clearer, you become still and you find your bearings again, irrespective of how windy or stormy it is.

Now, I want you to picture something. Imagine a miracle cure that makes your biggest problems in life go away. It's this amazing discovery which, when absorbed, can make your greatest pains and discomforts disappear. Now picture this cure compressed and synthesised into a capsule, like a vitamin. Except, in order for this one capsule to pack so much power and remedy, it has to be bigger than a normal sized capsule that you might be used to. This makes the pill hard to swallow. In fact, history shows that people usually choke on it and spit it out, missing out on the benefits packed away inside. For the people who do manage to get it down, they receive the benefits and their life, as they know it, changes.

The pill I'm talking about is called reality by some and truth by others. There will be plenty of that in this book. Not because I want to give you tough love but because it's what woke me up from my own personal haze and sleepwalking. It takes courage to choose to see your reality differently and it takes a degree of trust to step into a dark room that you know contains what you've been looking for.

Acknowledge your courage and trust in your ability to get yourself where you want to be. And know, that if you're reading this, a reality check is probably exactly what you need right now to help you grow beyond your current challenges, limitations and opportunities.

Let me lay this out for you. Your life, your perceptions and your beliefs are your responsibility. No one is responsible for the way you see yourself or the way you see the world, no one is responsible for what you believe and no one is responsible for the actions you take.

This truth is equally confronting and liberating simply because it implies that you have a choice. That's right, at any given moment in your life you get to choose what you perceive, believe and act on. This is your life, no one is going to live it for you, have your perceptions for you or take action for you. They can't—they're too busy wrestling with their own life. Take responsibility for your life before you continue on your journey with your compass. It will make for a fulfilling one.

How To Use This Book

This book has been written and organised so you can look up your present challenge and gain some insight into what led you to it, and what might be a wise way to navigate through it.

The chapters have been organised to collectively make sense if you were to read it cover to cover. It follows the natural progression that you might go through when dealing with various aspects of life. That's not the only way to read this book though. It's also been designed like a guide with multiple entry points.

The moment you turn the page and begin reading this book is the moment the book that I wrote becomes your book. I want you to make it your book. Write in the margins, add your notes, highlight, circle and underline what resonates with you. I wrote this book for you.

The insights, wisdom and knowledge in this book are not mine to claim. Throughout my life, I've borrowed many compasses from those who had one. Some are people alive in body and others alive in spirit. Masters of the past who have left their insights and wisdom in books and teachings. I've taken everything that I've learnt about life's journey from these great minds, mixed it with my experiences and turned it into the following pages. They helped me find my way, so now they, and I, get to help you do the same.

This book is your compass now. Take it with you through your life and come back to it as often as you need. I'm here in these pages for you whenever you need me. This book is here to help you find your bearings when you get lost and help you get back on path when you veer too far from the clearing.

Journeying through life without a compass makes for a confusing and disorienting voyage. Set off on your journey, just be sure to take your compass with you.

1 YOUR WORLD

"Know thyself."

TEMPLE OF APOLLO IN DELPHI (PLATO)

KNOW YOURSELF

After you've lived your life and everything is said, done and not done, were you successful at life?

This is the question you will most likely ask yourself in the later years of your life. You probably want to feel like you have lived successfully, whatever that means to you.

My version of success isn't what most people would initially pick.

To me, being successful means knowing who you are. To know yourself. Everything in life comes after that. If you know who you are, all of the other pieces of life come together with clarity. When you're uncertain and confused about who you are, you'll end up surrounded by more things that confuse you and leave you uncertain about what you want. Knowing who you are also helps you understand who you are not. It also makes decision-making simple because your inner compass knows which way is north.

Not knowing who you are is scary. I know this because I've been there myself. I spent years trying to work out who I was through what I chose as a career or vocation. This is a common path in a world where we define our identity by our active source of income. People pick a career path they think they want, and then somewhere down the path they realise they can't stand what they're doing anymore. This leaves them feeling empty inside, as Henry David Thoreau wrote brilliantly, "living a life of quiet desperation," not knowing where to go next.

What usually follows is known as an identity crisis. Which is when you've identified yourself with what you were doing, the job you were working in or the career you were building for yourself, then you wake up and realise it's not fulfilling you and decide you want to change what you're doing. Then the thought hits you, 'If I believed that being a [insert your role] made me who I am, then if I'm no longer a [insert your role], who does that leave me to be?'

This leaves you feeling like you're floating without gravity. Nothing is keeping you on the ground and you're not really floating away, you're just hanging in the void. No matter how much energy you put into trying to move, it doesn't get you anywhere. Like a hot air balloon unable to return to the ground or move higher into the jet stream. That's scary and can trigger surging amounts of anxiety.

I've experienced identity crises several times in my life. I went through it as I ended each stage of my professional life. The moment I found something to grab onto, I held on with tight fingers to make sure I wouldn't be hanging in that scary void again. At least I didn't let myself experience it for too long.

Being in that void is valuable. It's in the place you think you've lost yourself that you truly find yourself. You are found to the degree you are lost. Some people come out of the womb knowing who they are; for others, it takes realising they have no idea who they are to discover the truth of who they are at the level of their soul.

Think of it this way: if you're hanging in the void, with nothing to grab onto, what does that force you to do? Be alone with your *Self*. You have to confront who you are. You can't run from yourself when you're alone with no one but your *Self*. How can you know yourself if every waking minute you're doing something to consciously or unconsciously distract yourself from being alone with your thoughts?

Yes, I'm referring to being addicted to technology, being social, overworking at your day job or keeping busy. You're so caught up in plummeting down that rabbit hole of distraction that you forget that you don't know who you truly are. The moment there's a sixty-second gap of time, your phone is in your hand and you're scrolling, consuming and getting distracted. What if the next time there are sixty seconds staring you in the face, you stop, keep your hands empty and give your heart a chance to whisper something meaningful to you?

The distractions that you intentionally let into your life are drowning out the whispers of your heart. The thing with your heart (as well as your intuition and soul) is that it doesn't get louder, you've just got to make things quiet around it. That means making your head and your space quiet. You will come to learn that silence is a powerful antidote to many of life's troubles.

In a world that can't stop talking and throwing useful—and useless—information around, the only way for you to come to know yourself and have any chance of loving your complete and authentic *Self* is to be still and listen. Listen within. The whispers of your heart are there all the time, waiting patiently for the day you choose to shut up and listen.

Create more opportunities for your heart to speak and you'll come to know yourself on levels you had no idea existed within you. Life is a journey of coming to know yourself. You can take decades to get there or intentionally start today. The choice is yours, it always has been.

Time to discover your*Self*.

“Everything that irritates us about others can lead us to an understanding of ourselves.”

CARL G. JUNG

SEE THE REFLECTION AROUND YOU

Have you ever been seated outdoors at a cafe and several tables over there was someone wearing a watch that kept reflecting the sun in your eyes? It's just the way they keep moving their hands when they talk. It's annoying enough to bother you but not so intrusive that you feel righteous enough to tell them how to move their hands.

Well, the same thing is happening with personality traits and behaviour on a day-to-day basis in everyone's lives. Metaphorically speaking, you are surrounded by constant reflections of yourself in mirrors of all different kinds. Typically, these mirrors are people. Sometimes they are animals and other times they are machines—remember that time you started talking to your car or computer?

Being responsible is a vital action to getting by in life. It's even more crucial if you plan on making your life your own. Part of that responsibility is owning what you see in the outside world. That's right, owning it. The good, the bad and the ugly.

Story time — for a long time, for various reasons, I believed that most of the men in my life were not demonstrating behaviour worthy of replicating in myself. I saw these people harbouring qualities that I decided I didn't want within myself. This, dangerously, led me down a psychologically conflicted path. I wanted my life to turn out a certain way but didn't want to end up behaving like them in the process of creating that life. You may already see where this is going. I wanted a certain life for myself and I was convinced that I could do it without being anything like them.

As I worked out for myself and as I'd teach you, I had to own the things I was avoiding in order to get where I wanted. I had to pay the toll that I was avoiding to travel the road, you might say.

At the time I believed I was paying a toll, when in fact I was trying to find ways to travel the road without paying. Still, I believed I was paying a hefty fine for what I wanted. That was before I actually paid and before I realised how vital the fee was. When you realise the gift that you can unpack when you look directly into your reflection in others and own it, you'll learn that the fee is hardly a fee at all.

I'll ease you in with the nicer traits and qualities first. You know that person you look up to who has a quality about them that you admire? Well, that's a reflection that you're seeing. That sense of admiration, that sense of impression that lifts you a little when you interact with them, see them, hear them or read something of theirs, is actually you seeing a part of yourself that you haven't yet recognised. You've disowned that admirable part of yourself, so much so that the only way you'll see it is in others. You probably even say to yourself, "I wish I could be like them," or "there's no way I could be like them." What you don't realise is that you're saying, "There's no way I could be like me."

There was a scientific breakthrough in history when it was realised that light travels in cyclic waves. The speed of these waves is called frequency and is measured in hertz (Hz). The spectrum of light ranges from low frequencies that we can't see through the various colours and then beyond into higher frequencies that we can't see without electronic sensors – x-ray, gamma ray, radio waves, etc. The same is true for sound. It travels in waves, is measured in hertz (Hz) and the various frequencies determine how high or low the pitch is to the human ear. There is also a wide range of frequencies we can't hear – think of dog whistles. This is important to understand to help you realise just how much a reflection you're seeing around you.

There's a principle in acoustics called sympathetic resonance. If you have two tuning forks of the same note and hit one to make it vibrate with sound and bring it close to the silent tuning fork while it's still vibrating with sound, it will cause the silent tuning fork to vibrate and generate the same tone. This happens without physically touching the second tuning fork.

Another example of this is with guitars. If you pluck a string on one guitar and bring it close to another silent guitar, the same string that you plucked on the first guitar will begin to vibrate and generate sound on the second guitar. The examples of sympathetic resonance can go on and on. Take the opera singer who can shatter windows and crystal wine glasses when she reaches and holds a high note. She is singing at a resonant frequency that is the same as the natural structural frequency of the glass. It's all the same thing.

This is what happens with behavioural traits in others. When you're tingling with admiration and infatuation or burning with frustration and resentment, you're the tuning fork that hasn't been hit but is still vibrating. The person you're observing is vibrating, they're sending out waves and you're resonating at the same tone or frequency.

The same thing happens when you despise, resent or are frustrated by something in another person. You're resonating with what you're seeing and it's bringing up feelings you don't like or something stronger than "don't like". The fact of the matter is, either way, you're disowning what you're seeing. That sympathetic resonance or reflection is internal feedback attempting to wake you up to what you haven't yet owned within yourself. It's showing you that you're not willing to see yourself in the world that you're observing. You're being deflective, bouncing light away from you.

Just like it was true for me, it's true for you. To get where you want to go, to move further down your path, to move past being stuck, you are required to own and embody the traits you've been disowning.

It seems counter-intuitive but your ability to absorb the reflections you see means you're unable to be affected by them. Remember our friend in the cafe whose wristwatch was reflecting the sun in your eyes? Well, that's what all of your bothersome reflections are doing. Imagine everyone carrying around tiny mirrors reflecting the light directly into your eyes. They're trying to get your attention. They're trying to show you something you've been avoiding about yourself. Whether it's perceived as good or bad, you've been avoiding it and the reflection will continue to distract you until you're able to own it 100%. Only once you've owned your reflection can you embody more of yourself in a way that only few have mastered.

By enabling yourself to own what you see in the world around you, you will come to see that you have had everything you've ever needed within you this whole time. You will see that you haven't been missing anything inside of you, you've just been ignoring it. You've been disowning it. The good and the bad. Imagine that, everything you've been searching for out there has been pointing back to you.

You're not here to be only good without bad. You're here to be you, and that means being all of who you are, not just the parts you like. To add more irony, the more strongly you disown your parts, the stronger the reflections become around you. People will behave in ways that they don't usually behave in, strangers will reflect the behaviour and push your buttons, children will do things you don't expect or things that don't usually bother you will start to bother you. It starts to escalate.

The reflection will follow you around until you give it the attention it's seeking so you can own and embody what you see to the degree that you see it. It's designed to do that. When you're able to do that with the mirror that's being used to reflect light directly into your eyes, the person carrying that mirror will put it down as if to say, "Okay, you got it. I don't need to shine this in your eye anymore."

When you're able to see your reflection in the outer world and the outer world within, you will become more of the master you were meant to be. This is part of the journey to knowing yourself.

Another note on the subject of reflection: whenever you feel the pain, sorrow or emotions of another person, it's the same thing. They're reflecting your unresolved pain and emotion back at you. They're attempting to help you heal the unresolved pain you've been ignoring. This is also why you might experience movies vividly or be moved by characters in a story. You're seeing your reflection in the character you are empathising with. Again, what's being reflected on the cinema screen is a reflection of what's on the inside of your mental screen.

Think of your reflection in the world as a way for you to see yourself with perspective. When you stand in front of a mirror, you see parts of yourself you would've otherwise struggled to see or just completely missed. That's what the world is – your life-sized mirror, reflecting back at you parts of yourself you would've otherwise struggled to see. The world is helping you see yourself from different angles with crystal clear accuracy.

You think that you are the reflection you see in the mirror. You believe that what is looking back at you is who you are. But it's just that, a reflection. You are actually the source of light that is bouncing off the mirror in the first place. You are the light being projected onto the mirror, not what's being reflected off it. Recognise yourself as the source of light that you are. Instead of trying to change the projection, you can start changing what is doing the projecting.

When you recognise yourself in the mirror that surrounds you, your life will change. It's a way of reclaiming your power because the buttons that others used to be able to push no longer work. The power you once gave others is now yours to keep.

So now, when you look out at your reflection in the world around you, who do you see? Someone worthy of being reflected?

"Be careful how you interpret the world; it is like that."

ERICH HELLER

REWRITE YOUR BELIEFS

As we move through life, we develop beliefs or rules. These beliefs are compiled and used regularly both consciously and unconsciously. These beliefs are like pictures – snapshots of how you believe the world and you operate.

When I came to realise how beliefs are created, I came across something crucial to human behaviour and mindset. Just because you believe something doesn't make it true.

That may seem obvious but it has depth when you reflect on it. Just because you believe something doesn't make it true. What does that mean? It means just because you've carried a belief for your entire life doesn't mean that it is the absolute truth. It's a truth to you. It's something you deem to be true irrespective of whether nature or the universe you inhabit agrees.

The only reason you continue to carry that belief is because on some level it serves you. Otherwise, you'd throw it out and develop a new one.

When people tell me about their problem that seems insurmountable, I ask a variety of questions to determine their underlying belief and then help them drop the belief that is stopping them from getting where they want. In the process, a new belief is automatically founded in their mind, which enables them to move in the direction they choose. One belief stops serving them, and a new one replaces it.

How? Let's start with how beliefs are created in your mind.

At some point in your past you went through an experience and had a perception of that experience or event. Whether your perception was good or bad, it created a belief in your mind. You then jotted down that belief in your little mental book of rules and went on throughout your life testing to see if this belief was true.

As you continue through life, you'll come across experiences that have some similarity to that initial experience you had. When this happens, the first thing you do is pull out your book of rules, check to see if it's true and then confirm your findings. Now that you have your book out and you see

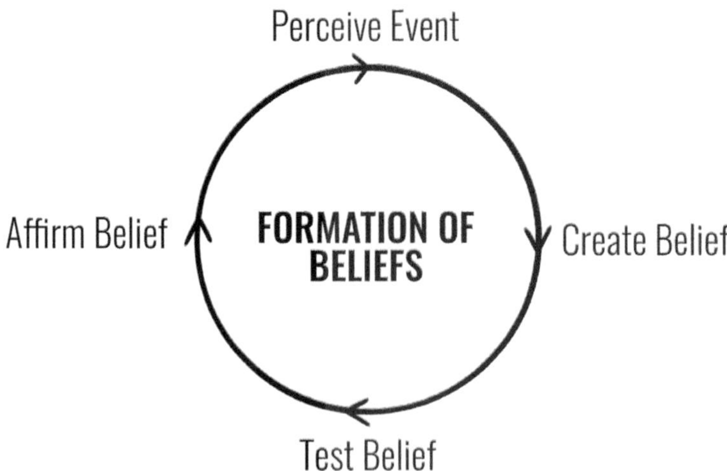

these two scenarios as similar, you respond to the current situation the same way you did the first time. As you make your way further down your journey, you keep adding more details and characteristics to your initial belief, which makes this belief a one-size-fits-all perception.

For example, let's say you develop a strong relationship with your dad as a child, but then he decides to leave and create a new life for himself. You take that personally, as in you think you're the reason he left and he rejected you. Moving forward, you keep men at arm's length because you have developed the belief that when you let people in, especially men, and allow them to get close, they will leave and hurt you. So in every experience after that belief-defining moment, you avoid getting close to men to safely avoid that pain.

Here's the interesting part. Because you believe that things will go a certain way, you create that very reality. You unconsciously behave or act in ways that create the outcome which confirms your initial belief. All of which reaffirms your belief and encourages you to believe it's true. Can you see the cycle? It's not some especially mystical voodoo.

The more you test the belief, the more characteristics you'll add to the belief and the more elaborate it becomes. This will continue to happen throughout your life unless you do one simple but powerful thing that few people are willing to do – question your beliefs and question them regularly. More on that later. For now let's take a deeper look at the effects your beliefs have on your life.

The effect of your beliefs

The diagram below demonstrates the effects of your beliefs. They have an immense ripple effect throughout all areas of your life. This means that changing them has an equally big impact on what you achieve in your lifetime.

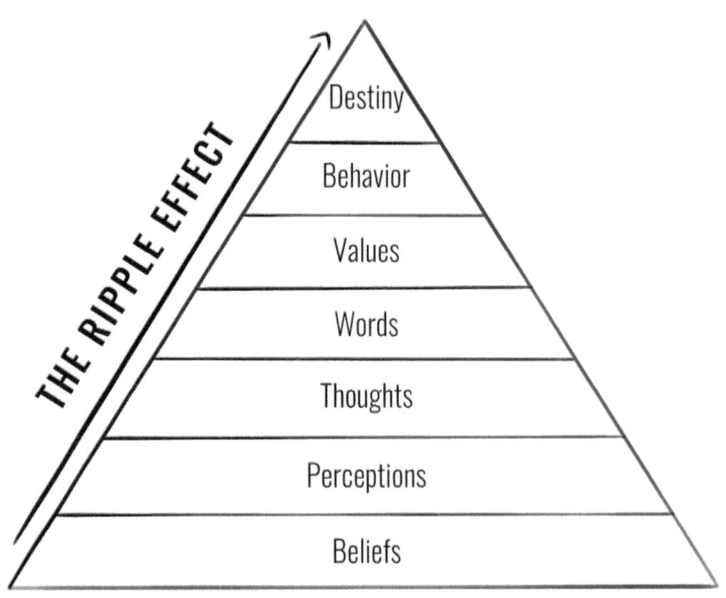

Beliefs → Perceptions → Thoughts → Words → Values → Behaviour → Destiny

Here lies a clue to why trying to change habits through force doesn't always work. The underlying belief that is driving the behaviour hasn't been changed. If you want to change your thoughts, words, behaviour, values or life, it's best to go to the root or source and change the belief. Focussing your attention there will have a ripple affect on the rest.

Think of your behaviour and destiny as the effect and your beliefs as the cause. Focus on the cause and it'll have an effect. If you want to reap fruit from the tree of your mind, you'll need to tend to the roots as well as the soil that the roots are planted in.

Here's an analogy which relates to dealing with the cause and not the effect.

Imagine you're chopping vegetables in the kitchen and you cut yourself with the knife. You stop, clean your wound and then pop a band-aid on it to help it heal. Then you go back to chopping the vegetables and cut yourself again in a different spot. Another band-aid and back to the chopping board.

You can keep doing the same thing and you'll keep going through band-aids. This will continue because you're not doing anything about the cause of the problem. You'll need to change the way you're chopping or use a different knife, instead of slapping band-aids on your fingers like it's a carnival game.

Continually putting band-aids on is like trying to change your behaviour or thoughts without altering your beliefs. It's temporary and it won't last. It's not sustainable in the long term.

Why? Because your beliefs sit in your unconscious mind. They've been stored there for efficiency. You've been believing them for long enough that they become second nature without any conscious thought required. It's as automatic as breathing, digesting, pumping blood and fighting infection.

Trying to change behaviour without changing your belief is like trying to hold your breath. You can put conscious effort into holding your breath but at some point, your unconscious mind will kick in and override your conscious mind, and you'll be gasping for air before you know it. Your unconscious mind will win – every time.[1] Instead of trying to overpower it, work with it.

The best way to start altering your beliefs is to ask questions. Questions that you haven't asked before, so you can uncover answers you haven't come up with before.

When you find something you want to change about your behaviour, answer some of these questions:

- What's getting in your way of what you want to achieve?
- What do you believe about that?
- When did you begin to believe that to be true?
- What happened back then that led you to believe that to be true?

---

[1]I am aware there are ways to train yourself to override your brain's autonomics so you can hold your breath for extended periods of time. Keep in mind though, people who have trained to do so have reported forgetting to breathe in normal situations because they've altered their unconscious response to what used to be automatic control.

- Could there be another truth to that experience? (If you answer no to this question, you're probably not ready to change the belief.)

Here's the deal. All of the consultations I've had with various people from all walks of life have resulted in me ultimately helping them change a belief they had about themselves or the world. The magic lies in simply finding and changing the belief that clashed with what they want.

Why do I do this? Because it's the fastest and most efficient way of changing your life. Remember that diagram on page 26? If you want to change your life, it's wisest to change the beliefs you have about your life. It's been the most powerful form of change I've ever created for myself and others.

Beliefs are your rule book for life and as long as you keep the same rules, you'll continue to play the same game the same way. If you want to play as batter in a baseball game but keep walking onto the pitch with a catcher's mitt, then you're not giving yourself a chance. That's fine if you like the game you're playing, but if you want to change the game you're playing, it's time to start changing your own rules about how to play the game.

You have a destination that calls you. Destiny is another word for destination. If you have a destination you're called to but your beliefs stop you from getting there, then the best place to start working through is your unconscious belief system.

Your beliefs don't make you who you are. They just determine how you see and respond to the world. Developing self-awareness will help you see your beliefs. You can't change what you can't see. By seeing your beliefs as they are, without judgment or attachment, you can then start to change them.

Seeing your beliefs means becoming consciously aware of them. Taking out the old dusty rule book, inspecting the pages, ripping out the ones that no longer serve you on your journey and writing new ones.

By being willing and able to change your beliefs you allow yourself to adapt to life, which makes you more prepared to deal with change. People's inability and unwillingness to change is a recurrent cause of challenge, tension and conflict in their lives.

Seeing your beliefs for what they truly are and then changing them equips you with a power that will change how you live your life.

Change your beliefs and you change your life. This chapter alone can change the trajectory of your life, permanently.

“It’s not what you look at that matters; it’s what you see.”

HENRY DAVID THOREAU

BREAK THROUGH YOUR ILLUSION

The word perspective comes from optics and means "to look through". It means that when we view the world and our experiences, what we really do is look through the lens of our perceptions.

As we grow up, we're taught to trust what we see. We believe what our senses are telling us. But what if your perceptions are incomplete? What if the world you're seeing, hearing and feeling is missing a vital part of the picture?

Your judgments of the world, whether positive or negative, directly impact what you see in each moment. But, is what you're seeing the whole truth and nothing but the truth? (I had to slip that in – I'm not sorry.)

You don't always realise it but you're filling in a lot of blanks with your assumptions. This can lead to a distorted view of what you're seeing and experiencing.

Consciously you can only take in so much information. You're filtering parts of your environment out to avoid the flood of information. This is a normal function and essential for your survival. But if misunderstood, it can work against your intentions. The filtering leaves your mind to fill in the gaps with assumptions. Meanwhile, your subconscious mind is taking in all of the detail. Think of it like a 360° camera – your unconscious mind – versus a standard point-and-shoot camera – your conscious mind. One of them is capturing everything, and the other is focussed on one particular point of view and usually on one subject within that limited view. They are different perspectives of the same thing.

So if you think of an experience you're having when someone is criticising you or being condescending in some way, you'll probably be so focussed on what that person is doing to you that it will distract you from everything else that's taking place around you, including what other people are doing or saying in that same moment. It just so happens that the 'hidden' stuff that you're not aware of is equally important for you to pay attention to.

Why is it equally important? Because in order for you to understand why things take place in your life, you'll need a balanced perspective of what's taking place.

When you're experiencing challenges in your life, you'll most likely ask the question, "Why is this happening?" It's difficult to reveal the answer to that question when you're emotionally charged up about what's happening. Bringing balance to your mind is what will help you uncover the answers. This is because bringing balance to your mind requires changing your perspective. It sounds simple and it is, which is why so many people don't do it.

However, don't confuse simple with powerless.

I explain more about balance in an upcoming chapter (page 39). For now, I want you to have an awareness that your perceptions aren't necessarily complete. Which also means that there are illusions you've been holding onto about past experiences, people, the world around you and, most importantly, yourself. As you uncover these illusions that you may or may not be aware of, you'll undoubtedly get angry and may even start to beat yourself up.

There's no value in doing that. Simply accept that you didn't know any better at the time. It's the equivalent of getting angry at a first-year medical student for not knowing how to remove an appendix. That's not fair, because they don't know any better in their infancy of knowledge. Give yourself a break and appreciate that you were doing what you knew to do at the time. Just like all of your peers on this gorgeous blue spaceship.

Back to your mind. If you're consciously filtering out your environment then what's your subconscious up to? Well, it's taking in everything and storing it. It's working away saying, "This is good, I'll put a 'good' label on it and file it away. Oh, this seems to be bad, I'll file that where it belongs." While you're going about your life, it's doing what it can to organise what comes in and to make sense of your experiences and thoughts. This is a simplified version of what's going on, but you get my point.

This is how you develop your beliefs and understanding of the world. But you're ignoring half of the perception. What if you started to explore your past and found that maybe what you once thought was challenging wasn't that bad, and that other thing you were excited about was actually causing you problems?

Well, your subconscious mind would need to do some reorganising, move things around, throw out some perceptions that are no longer useful and dig up others that prove to be more valuable than you initially believed.

This is the process of changing your beliefs. By changing your beliefs, you alter your response to life and your path. By doing this, you're altering your destiny (destination). Does that mean you would be taking your destiny into your own hands? Perhaps. I know one way for you to find out the answer.

“Things are made clear by their opposites. It is impossible to make anything known without its opposite.”

RUMI

RECOGNISE THE BALANCE OF IT ALL

Life has an abundance of opposites. It carries a balance of coupled polarities. Nature's balancing scale is constantly maintaining the difference between two sides of complementing opposites. It's keeping the delicate balance of opposites in a constant state of equilibrium.

This can seem obvious once it's understood, but it's something that is easily overlooked and avoided as a teaching. The poles of opposites exist in many places in life:

Hot/Cold
Life/Death
Fear/Courage
Summer/Winter
Fast/Slow
Begin/End
High/Low
Push/Pull
Gain/Loss
Strength/Weakness

North/South and East/West
Happy/Sad
Pride/Shame
Light/Dark
Up/Down
Attract/Repel
In/Out
Close/Distant
New/Old
Positive/Negative

Agonist/Antagonist	Excess/Deficiency
Creation/Destruction	Tear-down/Build-up
Financial boom/Financial bust	Bear market/Bull market
Debt/Profit	Methylation/Acetylation
Anabolism/Catabolism	Expand/Retract

What I want you to recognise is that all opposites are relative. Consider the poles of hot and cold. They rest at either end of their own scale. They are polar opposites with varying degrees in between. But where does one end and the other begin? There's no official beginning of cold and end of heat or vice versa. Everyone has their own opinion of where hot starts and cold starts, but as you get closer to either of the two extremes, it becomes more and more obvious. It becomes more definitive, more contrasting, more evident. How does this apply to life though?

Your ability to perceive hot and cold, light and dark, happy and sad is within the realm of your mind. Your mind's ability to receive information, interpret it and use it is a powerful function.

Stop and think about that for a moment. You have the ability to perceive a sliding scale of extremes. This isn't some random bet that evolution made and won somewhere in the past. It's important for more than just survival. It's what makes your existence and journey a whole other experience.

For added perspective, imagine yourself as a visitor to earth. You have no personal association with this place, you're just here because you heard it was an interesting place to experience so you decided to try it out. You arrive, not entirely aware of why things happen or how things happen, and you want to learn something new. So you travel the globe. You observe people, you observe nature, you observe the way life unfolds here but you have no real ability to personally identify with anyone or anything. You're on the outside looking in.

What you may notice in your travels is that people are caught up in their smaller versions of existence. They've been building a story of themselves and of the world around them since they were born. They're so personally involved in what they see that it's impossible for them to not take things personally. What happens as a result of them taking things personally? They form judgment in the mind. They mentally label things as good or bad, right or wrong, nice or cruel, beautiful or ugly. Now, because you're a visitor and are not emotionally invested in what they judge, you just see their world as it is.

You see their world as a finely tuned balance of good and bad, right and wrong, nice and cruel, beautiful and ugly. Your view is neutral. You see it as neither and both.

Now, have you heard the saying, "One man's rubbish is another man's treasure?" That's the essence of perception. What some will judge as good, others will judge as bad. What some consider bad, others will consider a blessing. Whatever perspective the individual holds, they believe it is valuable. That's the only reason they'd hold onto their view.

I'll give you another example using temperature again. Suppose you decide to bake a loaf of bread. To bake the bread you'd be setting the oven temperature somewhere around 200°C (392°F). This temperature seems extreme compared to a hot summer's day of 43°C (110°F). The oven temperature for baking bread is like a cool bath to a blacksmith or metalworker who is operating furnaces of 1600°C (2912°F). Different people will see these various temperatures as hot or cool based on their perception. They may have been conditioned to think a certain way but that's because of their perception – their gauge of things.

So how does the balance of opposites come into play? Well, this see-sawing scale of perception impacts the way you see the world. You may see getting fired from your job as a terrible situation whereas your partner might feel great about it because you'll stop complaining about your job. One person's adversity is another person's opportunity. Your adversity is also your opportunity.

The opposite can take place too. You may have just signed on a million-dollar client but you may have to give up watching movies with your family or going out to social dinners so you can serve the client effectively. You see more income, but your partner or friends might see less social time together. It's the same situation that everyone is experiencing, but each person will have a different perception and therefore a different judgment of it.

So the grand question you might have is, who is right and who is wrong? I won't answer that, I'm not here to discuss morals. Here's what I will say though. You get to choose. If you want it to be a bad situation then it will be that; if you want it to be a good situation then that's what it will be. If you want to see it as both, good and bad, equally, then you will see something substantially different. You will see the truth of the situation. You will see it for what it truly is and you'll wake up to the inherent value of it.

In a lot of psychology and self-help texts you'll find that there is a focus on either good or bad perceptions. They mostly talk about how people see things on either end of the scale, but they don't talk about the gap between the two extremes. More specifically, they don't talk about the exact centrepoint between the two ends. They don't talk about the good and bad aspects of life being equal, having equal value, weight and importance to one another.

Why is this important? Well, if you knew that life was filled with equally good and bad experiences then wouldn't that mean that at any moment you have the power to choose how you want to see something? Doesn't this mean that you're free to change your perception of yourself, the people around you and the experiences you have? Wouldn't it mean that you're not a victim of your life but more powerful than you first believed?

This may conflict with your beliefs and that's okay. It may also be blatantly obvious to you, which is more likely. Either way this single truth, this one principle of nature, may very well be the most profound thing you learn about life and your place in it.

Consider a flower. I have friends who struggle with hay fever who don't like flowers because of their physical reaction to them. To my wife, however, flowers are beautiful and fragrant. They are a sign of the cycle of seasons and the life that is reviving from the cold of winter. Has the flower been or done anything? No, it's just a flower. But two people have two opposing perceptions of this flower, while the flower is being neutral.

Just because you perceive something to be good or bad does not make it so. Neutrality is truth, it's objective. It is the glue that holds every complementary opposite together, including perceptions within the mind.

If you look again at the balancing scale of good and bad, you can see that at different moments in your life you would have felt that it was tipped more one way than the other. You would have had times when it seemed impossible to lift the bad side up or when the happiest moment in your life couldn't have possibly been balanced out with bad. And as long as you believe this to be true, you keep the scale locked into its lopsided position. You keep your perceptions and beliefs anchored and fixed in a world that is constantly changing around you. This is also why people struggle with change. Adapting to the world requires a willingness to change your perceptions.

So what happens when you take a positive or negative perception and balance it out with its opposite? What's the point of getting the good and bad of something to equal each other? Well, that's where the magic happens. When you balance out the way you perceive the world around or within you, you wake up to something that is hiding beneath the surface.

There's a truth waiting to be seen and the only way you're going to gain access to it is by getting your mind to see both sides equally. To achieve true neutrality. The moment you see a bad experience as equally good or a good situation as equally bad, you wake up what some people call a feeling inside that can move mountains. That feeling has many names, but most commonly gets referred to as gratitude, thankfulness, appreciation and, sometimes, love.

Why does it take perceiving a balance of both to be the key to experiencing gratitude? Because when you balance your perception and your view, you open yourself up to seeing the truth of what you're looking at. It opens you up to see that it's as it's meant to be, not how you wish it to be. It is exactly what it is, as it is, and once you see the whole picture, you can then influence its change. Paradoxically, the only true way to change something in your life is to first see that it's perfect and doesn't require change. Getting there requires true neutrality.

I know, it's a lot to take in. And may seem even harder to apply. This is all really intellectual and thought-provoking.

The application of this principle to different parts of your life will be where you see exactly what I'm referring to. Reading this chapter and thinking, "Oh yeah, I see what he's saying" isn't enough. That's the equivalent of smelling a glass of wine and saying that you've tasted it. You haven't really experienced the taste of it, you've just gotten a sense of what it tastes like.

If all things in life are balanced, then what's the point of it all? What are we experiencing? There are deep answers to that question that I cannot do justice to in one paragraph, but I will say one thing. Whatever you experience in your life is exactly what you're meant to experience at that time. It's meant to be everything that it is for you until you're ready to see it in a different light. Only then will you be able to dig deeper into what importance that experience has in your journey. Those of you who have experienced varying degrees of trauma may disagree, and I understand where you're coming from. But know this: I don't say what I've said lightly, nor do I say it without having factored you in. Your trauma is not exempted. It's included.

For me, and for many giants of history, life has had a hidden order lying beneath the surface. Call it what you will, but there is something there that's cutting through the apparent chaos of life. This is where a balance of opposites finds its place.

Think about it. If negative or bad experiences didn't serve some kind of purpose, why would they take place at all? As a species keen on avoiding pain – emotional or physical – does it not pique your curiosity about why these apparently bad things take place? Maybe they serve the equally important role of maintaining a balance of opposites, to ensure life doesn't run too far off into one extreme.

Personally, I don't have anything to gain by making you agree with this principle. You stand to learn something valuable that you can't unlearn. This is an opportunity for you to equip yourself with knowledge and wisdom about life that won't ever be taken away from you. More profoundly and importantly, you have the opportunity to use this principle as a way for you to choose how you see life from moment to moment.

You get to choose. One of the most powerful statements ever said to another individual. With that power to choose comes your responsibility to live your life. Your life, no one else's, the one you were gifted with.

Your life has been and will be filled with good and bad equally. Balancing out your mind from either extreme on the scale will help calm your mind, enlighten your heart and open you up to the real potential that you are submerged in at every moment.

You've been swimming in the oceans of opportunity your whole life. But if you keep telling yourself that you're drowning, then you will never slow the panic down long enough to see what it is you're actually surrounded by – an astounding life filled with a delicate balance of opposites. Or as I like to describe it – perfection.

"The universe does not waste a single quark; all serves a purpose and fits into a balance — there are no extraneous events."

DAVID R. HAWKINS, M.D., PH.D.

LOOK TO NATURE FOR ANSWERS

From a young age — around five — I questioned the purpose of certain aspects of life. I asked authorities — parents — for answers, which they were only able to provide with limited certainty. That is, when they weren't dismissing me in their busyness of raising three children. When I wasn't able to get satisfying answers from them, I turned to religious texts. Again, unable to find clearcut answers, I was left frustrated, anxious and confused. It didn't stop me though; I was on a mission.

I had this burning desire within me to find the answers to "Why is this happening?" that actually satiated my curiosity instead of responses like, "That's just life" or "You win some, you lose some." Whenever something bad happened to me or someone close to me, I would think to myself, "This must've happened for a reason. Surely, it wouldn't have been something that is purely random?" I wasn't set on making religion the answerer of my inquiries but I was determined to find answers one way or another. Even if it meant exploring theology.

Then after years of struggling with myself and life, I came across the idea that nothing in this life exists without a purpose. My reaction was, "I knew I wasn't making it up!" Try to find something in the natural world that doesn't serve a purpose to the greater existence of the collective. You won't. Each and every part has a purpose. This is because anything unnecessary is made redundant.

Nature documentaries showing a wild pack of lionesses hunting down a wildebeest might make you momentarily feel bad for the wildebeest but then you almost instantly rationalise the scene with, "That's just the circle of life." So why then are people instantly victimised into their circumstances when someone endures 'bad, terrible or horrible' events? Is it because it's socially acceptable for the friends of the said victim to sympathise, victimise and enable the prey's thinking? Is anyone thinking or asking, "Well, that must've happened for a reason. Surely that didn't happen out of complete and utter randomness?"

I know there are some of you reading this who are about to throw this book across the room, in the rubbish bin, out the window of a ten-storey building or straight into the fireplace. Before you do, let me make something clear. I'm not writing what I've written without experience. I don't write it without having personally gone through my own myriad of challenges, along with having helped a growing number of people through their physical and psychological traumas.

I'm also not going to run through a list of experiences and the hidden reason for why they happen, like a list of symptoms and their remedies. Each person's specific experience of life and the circumstances that life has put them through are exactly that: specific. Your experiences are specific to you, and important for you and your life trajectory.

Back to the experiences that you've gone through. There was some reason for you, at that time in your life, to go through what you went through the way you did. Otherwise, why would it have happened?

Why would something happen if there was no reason for it? Why would something exist if it had no purpose? I ask the same question of experiences, events, people, emotions, thoughts, beliefs, and even symptoms or 'dis-ease' in the body. Why would any of the above, positive or negative, exist if they had no purpose to serve?

Some people come up with the easy answer. "They're just random. There's no calculation hidden behind them. There's nothing driving all of this other than a cosmic roulette game taking place." To me, that's a cop-out and a way for people to shelter themselves from feeling pain. If that's you and you have no interest in seeing life any differently, put the book down. Trust me, you're not going to like the rest of it.

If you're still reading, I suspect you've felt the same way I have for a very long time. You believe that things in life happen for a reason. That there must be some meaning or purpose for the way your life has unfolded and the way you've experienced what you have so far. It's true. And the more I talk with clients, the more certain I am of this truth.

By nature, I have been deeply called to investigate the human experience of life. Band-aid answers never worked for me, whether I was questioning theology, what happens after death, why the body experiences dis-ease, why people argue, why people make decisions, why people experience emotions, why 'tragedies' happen and many, many more questions. The search for answers gets me out of bed every morning. And if I have these questions, then surely others do too.

I've been obsessed with finding meaning and purpose throughout life. Because of many childhood anxieties I experienced, I kept looking for meaning and purpose to see if I could ease my anxieties about life and how it unfolded. I had no idea I would actually come across the law of redundancy in nature. Once I understood it, I tested it out whenever I could on whatever I could.

So here I am today writing to you, telling you that amidst what you might call terrible incidents in life, I have yet to experience anything myself that I haven't been able to find some meaning or purpose to. The same is true of the lives that have been presented to me by those seeking my help.

When I talk about this natural law with others, I get a mixed response. Something between "I knew everything happens for a reason," and "You mean to tell me that everything, including the shit in life, has a purpose?"

After long conversations discussing the potential purpose of hypothetical situations, which is almost impossible to do, they leave our conversations on the resigning comment, "There's no way it all has a purpose. Especially the bad stuff." That's their way of saying that there's too much pain lurking beneath the surface of what they experience for them to want to go looking for any meaning.

To me, there are two groups of people when it comes to this topic of purpose. There are those who're looking for answers and those who aren't ready to ask the question. Neither are judgment-worthy.

The point is, if something serves no purpose or has no meaning, it is made redundant. There is so much beneath the surface of what is experienced in life, our cosmos, in our universe. It takes a growing degree of trust in this idea for you to be able to put the pieces of your life together as you venture down your journey. Reading these words won't be enough for you to believe in the idea but holding this in the back of your mind as you make your way through this book and throughout your life will add a touch of depth to what you experience that will never be taken away from you. Looking at life through this lens will change the life that you're looking at.

"If [the] power of balance were shifted the slightest degree, the whole system of the universe would become quickly reduced to a mass of inert matter."

NAPOLEON HILL

UNDERSTAND WHAT HOLDS LIFE TOGETHER

This chapter is going to push buttons for some of you and make total sense to others. There are many words that people have built a stigma around. The word *god* alone can trigger all kinds of biblical imagery in the mind of many of you. I'll do my best to not get into a debate on theology in this chapter because it's a major point of contention for most people and will dilute the effectiveness of what I'm trying to share.

My intention here is not to argue the name, characteristic appearance or the beginning point of life itself. I merely intend to present a notion that life is being guided or balanced, if you will, by some form of intelligence greater than our human comprehension. This chapter alone certainly won't be enough to do the subject justice. Nonetheless, I'll attempt using words to demonstrate what I'm referring to.

Have you ever wondered out loud or quietly inward, "Why is this happening?" You know those times in your life where one thing after the next seemed to work against you? No matter how hard you tried, how much effort you put in, it felt as though life was kicking you while you were down. It's almost like it happened on purpose. As if you were being taught a lesson that you didn't know you signed up for. Naturally, you'd probably say to yourself something along the lines of, "Well, it must be happening for a reason." Or "Things are just the way they're meant to be." Or "It is what it is."

What if these statements were all true? What if there was something at play much bigger than you and I can comprehend? What if there was something that was greater than the sum of all things and also within the essence of all things, maintaining a delicate but fundamental balance between the opposites of life?

We're all aware that there's a balance that exists in life. In some cases this balance is obvious, in others it is subtler but it is ever-present. I've written about this in the chapter on balance (page 39). I'm not the first to talk about this balance. It's not a revelation. It's not some breakthrough in human consciousness. There have been others before me who have done a better job explaining this balance than I have, and I'm sure there'll be more to come after me who describe it with greater detail. What isn't always mentioned is what is managing or maintaining that balance.

Balance has been described using objects like pendulums, seesaws, spinning tops and scales. These all make sense. They weigh an item against its complementary opposite, adding or subtracting weight to show that the measures are equal. While balance is important, what I'm talking about here is the middle point: the pivot where the pendulum is swinging from, the fulcrum of the seesaw and the scale or the tip of the spin top. These are the zero-points of the scale. The neutral point of the balance. The point that both sides rest and rely on. Their centre.

What would happen if this point, where the opposites meet, did not exist? What would happen if it was removed? The scales would collapse, the spin top would have nothing to spin on and the pendulum would have nothing to swing from. This thing that is holding everything in place is what I'm writing about here. The Grand Design, the order governing the chaos, the innate or infinite intelligence that permeates all things. The space *between* everything we know that *connects* everything we know and beyond. I can hear how that sounds, but I've witnessed this intelligence more often than most people and it humbles me every time.

Facing the death of loved ones as well as my own experiences with anxiety and depression drove me to question if there was something else going on beyond what my senses were capable of interpreting. There were questions that religion couldn't answer or would contradict itself when it tried to. There were also questions that science would refuse to entertain because to the scientific world they were not worth proving or disproving. So I explored other topics while I tried to work out my life.

I wasn't able to work life out very effectively, because the thing that I wanted answers about was the very thing that was going to help me make sense of it. The irony, as you'll learn in the pages of this book, was that the thing I was running from – finding meaning and purpose in life – was what was going to help me understand life in new and meaningful ways.

To me, life seemed chaotic. The events and experiences I was having weren't adding up. Life wasn't making sense to me. I struggled to find the order that I'm referring to. I believed there was order to be found, but I didn't know how to find it or where to look. Think of the old needle in the haystack analogy. Before you go digging for the needle, you must first believe the needle exists. Otherwise what are you digging for? The proverbial needle is the order in the apparent chaos of life. What appears to be just another chaotic haystack to most people conceals a hidden needle to the wise ones.

The reason I talk so strongly about an organising force that's much bigger than you and me is because of how much of it I've personally witnessed. I'm not parroting what someone has told me on blind faith. I talk from my years of experience helping people consistently find the needle in the haystack of their overwhelming challenges. No matter how chaotic their situation seems, they find order, organisation and meaning beneath it all every time. As if there was some hidden intention hiding beneath the surface of their chaos. This has been true for all sorts of experiences and events that people have encountered, from traumatic to seemingly meaningless. They all harbour meaning, purpose and order.

The good and bad in all aspects of life have a reason or purpose for existence, no matter how small and insignificant; otherwise, they'd be made redundant. So if that is true for everything and there indeed is hidden order within all of life, then surely that's being managed by something bigger than us. Something bigger than any supercomputer, and bigger than any collective group of people. Maybe it's so vast that it cannot be measured yet. Maybe it's so vast it's almost impossible to comprehend through logic and reason. Maybe this organised intelligence is infinite. An infinite intelligence, you might say.

This intelligence seems to defy the human odds, it seems to break the laws of man and the rules we've created. It seems to govern nature irrespective of what we believe to be right or wrong. That's the point. What you once believed was good and right has become bad and wrong. A perfect example of this is the experience of parents. The things they did as a young adult, they thought were right and good, but they believe those same actions to be bad and wrong for their own children. This works the other way too. What you once thought was bad and wrong becomes good and right. This is because the laws that people choose to govern themselves by are rarely in alignment with nature.

Fear, pride, shame and guilt are all reasons we struggle to live by nature's laws. Your best chance at navigating life with any sense of fulfilment and purpose is by aligning yourself with the laws of nature as best as you can. You may never align yourself completely but you can get yourself as close as possible.

It has also been liberating for leaders, CEOs and individuals of humble beginnings. This order and organisation that I'm talking about is something that's difficult to argue with when you see and experience it for yourself. It's been the single most liberating thing people I've worked with have experienced. These are people who endured what you might call trauma, abuse and violence, both physical and mental. It's been the principle and law that has freed me from most of my own turmoil and struggles in life. Realising and appreciating that nature or the universe knows more than I do has helped me wake up from the illusion I was living in.

In a way, this whole book is a demonstration of that hidden order of life. It's an example of how the weight of one side of the scales is balanced out by the weight of its complementary opposite. It is proof that both sides are created and maintained equally, that both sides have meaning and purpose for existence. No matter how much conscious effort you put into believing otherwise, you can't impede the laws of nature that dictate this conservation of balance. Any suffering you've experienced has happened because you've resisted this underlying order.

The beautiful irony here is that whenever we attempt to influence the laws that dictate this balance, we cause ourselves pain and struggle, then we blame this on external sources. The laws of nature don't change for us. We are no exception to the laws of nature. We are deeply a part of nature, but to become a master of your life you must first realise you are an apprentice. That's the cruel truth. But is it actually cruel? Is it as bad as it seems on the surface? Or are we just interpreting this truth of balance as a personal attack on our own existence? You know the answer to that. Become nature's apprentice.

Nature has been in operation longer than you and I have been in existence. It's been running the show long before we showed up. Maybe it knows a thing or two about how to govern life, including us within it. Maybe it is keeping all things in order, in balance and organised to a degree that can be difficult to comprehend intellectually. But it's easy to appreciate when it's inspected more directly with your own experience of life.

I won't do it justice in one chapter. This order, this law of nature, this conservation of balance has been written about by greater minds than mine in more poetic and understandable ways. So instead of re-inventing the wheel and attempting to do something as grand as universal law any justice, I would love you to see it as a demonstration of the universal laws that govern us and all other things too. See it as a case study, my own personal experience with the truth that every haystack has a needle hiding within it. As you read on, suspend whatever belief you have of life, the world and your experience. Allow yourself to momentarily believe that this haystack you've been lumped with contains a needle worth searching for.

It will take some time and exponential amounts of effort but when you find that needle nothing else will matter. The pain, the struggle and the hurt will instantly melt away and you'll appreciate what you've found. The needle is always there, waiting to be found by you.

So, when you look at your haystack, do you see dried grass or the potential for something more hiding inside?

2

YOUR MIND

“The outer work can never be small if the inner work is great. And the outer work can never be great if the inner work is small.”

MEISTER ECKHART

DEVELOP YOUR SELF-AWARENESS

All aspects of this book are in some way here to help you develop and sharpen your self-awareness. I could easily just suggest that you refer to all of the other chapters for self-awareness but that would be cheating my way out of writing some more.

Be warned, this will get quite abstract. Stay with me, it'll make sense by the end.

You are you, and the world is the world with all its parts. You seem to have the ability to distinguish yourself from things outside of you. You call those borders that separate you from the outside world as the "self". It makes navigating this physical reality a little bit easier. Without getting into the depths of who you are, I will say this: You are made up of a perfect balance of parts all coexisting together in an entangled harmony. This unique concoction of character and beliefs gives you a place in this universe.

A lot of your peers will live their lives in a manner of ignorance. They ignore themselves and don't really understand the depths of their character. There's nothing wrong with that. Their way of thinking is just as important as yours. But you're not them if you're reading this book and more specifically this chapter. You're here because you want to understand your "self" more deeply. You want to develop a self-awareness that fortifies your whole being.

Let me add to that by telling you that you're not who you say you are. Meaning, the things you say about yourself to others or the image of yourself you have in your mind is not definitively you. They're parts of you – fragments. Moments of time where you behaved in certain ways. They don't define you, they're comprised of parts of you. You are actually more than who you say you are and that's important to remember.

As I've mentioned in the chapter on reflection (page 15), what you see in people are the fragments of yourself that you're not fully aware of. As you go through life, you will slowly expand the way you see yourself and what you see in yourself. Think of being dropped into an area that you have no bearings of. You've been given a map with a dot in the middle indicating where you are, the rest is blank. As you venture away from the dot, you have to map out the area. Initially, you'll get help from others shaping the environment with you and showing you things you may not have seen. Then, as you become more confident in venturing further out, you begin to map areas completely on your own.

The metaphor here is that your parents and family will initially help you understand who you are, and then as you get older, you'll come to understand more about yourself. The more of life you explore and experience and the more people you interact with, the more you'll learn about yourself.

Where a lot of people become complacent is in trusting the map. Did you ever go back over the details of the map and check to see how accurate it is? Did you ever reassess the areas closest to the dot in the middle? Do you occasionally go back out to someplace you discovered to see if it's changed or if it was really the way you remember it?

These questions lead to self-awareness. Just because you think you know who you are, and you think you know what you're capable of, does not mean it is true or that you cannot change.

When I was in my early teens, I used to believe that the only way to change was through force and effort. If I wanted to do something consistently and habitually, I would try to force myself into it, but that didn't always work for me. It wasn't until I was able to change the way I saw myself, through self-awareness, that I was able to change my thinking and behaviour. Using the method of force and effort was harder because, while I was doing that, I was still holding onto thinking I knew who I was.

That kind of thinking makes it almost impossible to create change. Like pulling on an elastic band. The moment you let go of one side, it snaps back to wherever the other end is anchored. By freeing the other end of where it was being anchored to, the elastic band has more freedom to move.

Beware, you can very well tip the scale of self-awareness towards becoming self-obsessed. This manifests itself as bringing all conversations back to you somehow. You know people like this. No matter who is telling what story, they somehow manage to bring it back to them. This can happen internally when you venture beyond self-awareness into self-obsession. You'll know you're becoming self-obsessed when people stop telling you stories, when they stop opening up to you about their life and you may even find yourself lonely as a result. It will happen to you at some point, just be aware of finding a balance without swinging the pendulum too far.

Developing self-awareness begins by giving yourself the chance to rethink who you believe you are. It means letting go of what you think you're capable of and not capable of. It means momentarily lifting the boundaries of what you define yourself by. It's the chance you can give yourself to think, behave and live differently just by letting go of what you thought you knew about yourself. That's when you become aware of your "self".

Change where the elastic band is anchored by becoming aware that there is an elastic band in the first place.

"Our strength grows out of our weakness."

RALPH WALDO EMERSON

USE YOUR WEAKNESSES

If there's one thing I'm most certain of, it's that we all have weaknesses as much as we have strengths. A fool would think otherwise and would certainly believe that they can eliminate weaknesses in favour of strengths. I'm going to lean on history for a moment here. If you take the time to go and thoroughly study any individual who has made some kind of an impact on society – big or small – you will find they had weaknesses equal to their strengths just as you and I have.

Searching for someone who only has strength without weakness will result in a life wasted searching for the impossible.

So why is it important to confront and accept your weaknesses? Let me show you.

Who you are as a whole person is made up of a specific variety of parts. A perfect combination of pieces that fit together to make the complete you. Just like the cells, organs, connective tissue, bones, cartilage, hair and skin that all fit together to make your complete body.

It's the perfection of a stormy paradise that combines all parts of who you are – the strong and the weak, the profound and the profane, the inspiring and the frustrating, the intimidating and the nurturing – that makes you so unique and valuable.

If you think that only the good or nice parts make you, you, then you're deluding yourself into thinking that a puzzle with only half its pieces will complete the whole picture.

You're not half a jigsaw puzzle. You are the whole thing. Each and every piece is what makes you who you are.

Here's where things get messy about who you are. It's likely that if you're reading this chapter, you're the kind of person to go after the approval of others. Particularly the approval of people that you believe have their lives together, the people you feel have no weaknesses. You may be doing it consciously or unconsciously, but nonetheless, you're doing it. This desire for approval from those you look up to is a way of asking someone else, who you believe possesses traits you don't have, to say, "You are enough."

Let me tell you now: no amount of approval from others will ever make you believe that you're enough. That is something for you to validate from within. That is something for you to see and believe wholeheartedly. The way I've seen people do this most successfully is by confronting, accepting and appreciating their weaknesses as a vital part of the complete puzzle. Without your weaknesses you're incomplete.

Think about it. To be able to see your weaknesses as part of who you are as much as you see your strengths, means you are able to self-validate. It creates the space for you to be able to self-appreciate and for you to believe with all that you're made of that you are enough as you are. No one more and no one less.

Take a closer look and inspect a part of yourself that you believe to be a weakness. Ask yourself why you think that to be a weakness. Then look more closely at it and ask yourself how that weakness is actually a strength.

Please do not mistake this as positive thinking or an attempt to positively shift your mind. It's an attempt at getting you to see yourself in a more integrated and complete way. To help you experience a sense of wholeness by seeing both your strengths *and* weaknesses. It's a way for you to be able to admit to yourself that you do have weaknesses and that it's okay to have them. This isn't a way to ignore, deny or delude yourself into thinking that you have no weaknesses. That right there is a sure way to fall from grace. Just look at the mightiest leaders who fell from their height of ignorant power.

Let me give you an example of a young man named Leon. He struggled with self-worth and saw himself as a weak individual. This made it hard for him to function in the cut-throat industry of finance. In one session we went digging and found that he saw himself as having weaknesses that he believed needed fixing. He saw himself as a coward who ran away from challenges when they got too hard.

As we explored and dug through his beliefs, we came across a time when he was a young boy at soccer training. He was playing in a field position that he didn't like and felt weak in. He saw that he was unable to perform well in that role and chose to step into goal keeper position instead. The way he saw himself in his mind, however, as someone running away from what was a difficult position, and so he judged himself as being a coward.

So we did what I suggested above. I asked him to look for the strength he carried in that moment. To find where his strength was. To find where his courage was.

The words that I knew would come from his mouth are as important for you as they were for him. He realised that he was confronting his weakness by admitting he couldn't play in that role. He was confronting that he knew he wasn't strong in the position he was in. It took courage to admit that weakness to himself and to do something about it.

Let me be more direct for you. To admit that you have weaknesses and to do something about that takes courage, humility and strength. The trap that you've caught yourself in is you punishing yourself for having weaknesses. Having weaknesses is not punishment worthy. It's normal; in fact, it's natural and it's important for you to have weaknesses because, without them, you would not know the ups and downs of life. You wouldn't learn about yourself and you would miss out on the opportunity to connect and relate to the rest of the world, making it a lonely existence.

Looking at your weaknesses, confronting them and wholeheartedly appreciating them within you will be the source of your strength, power and self-worth.

Do not throw away half of the jigsaw pieces. Without them, you won't ever be complete. Without them, you won't ever get to see the grand picture of who you are. You won't get to see all of the marvellous and detailed parts that make you the unique complete puzzle that you are. Go and find the pieces you've tried to hide. What you'll see when you're done is something to marvel at. Believe me.

"Your vision will become clear only when you can look into your own heart. Who looks outside, dreams; who looks inside, awakes."

CARL G. JUNG

DISCOVER YOUR STRENGTHS

Firstly, I want you to know this important piece of information – there's nothing 'wrong' with you. Yes, I said it, and I'll continue to say it until you believe me. This whole book is aimed at showing you this truth. You can deny it all you like but as long as you're reading any page in this book, you will be continually exposed to the truth that you're not broken.

So where do your strengths come from? What is their origin? Where do they live within you and what does it take for them to come out and play? The answer isn't obvious – hence why most people struggle. It's common to think the way to strengthen something is by fixing, changing and filling in its weaknesses, as if each weakness is a hole that needs to be filled. It's not.

Time for an analogy. Think of your strengths and weaknesses as a mountain range. There are rolling hills of various sizes, climbing to different heights. And summits building upon summits that climb to peaks of incredible magnitude. And what is in-between these mountains? What lies between the peaks? What surrounds the range of mountains and hills? Valleys – or what you might call weaknesses. Are they truly weaknesses though?

It's somewhat normal for people to want to eliminate weaknesses because they're viewed as a fault, something bad or a defect of some kind. Well, if that were true, then we should go around and fill all of the valleys with enough dirt and soil to raise the ground level to the height of the mountain peaks, right? It sounds ridiculous but that's what fixing weaknesses looks like. Why am I talking about weaknesses in a chapter about strength? Because if you're thinking about strengths, you're probably thinking about eliminating weaknesses. You can read more about what to do about your weaknesses in the previous chapter (page 71).

By focussing on what's wrong with you, you are by default minimising your strengths. Believe it or not, they exist, but you can't see them because you're focussed on the defects. Your strengths are sitting patiently waiting for you to acknowledge them, waiting for you to look at them and smile with a warm, welcoming embrace. Your strengths are being loyal to you, they're a part of who you are, yet you've been ignoring them like a parent ignores a child they're ashamed of.

You've ignored these qualities about yourself because you've taken them for granted. There's even a part of you that has said, "I'm sure everyone does the same thing." They don't. They don't think like you, they don't live like you, they don't talk like you and they don't love like you. They have hearts and minds of their own.

So how do you honour strengths in your life? Firstly, become aware of them. When you realise this, you won't have to do much else, because they've been there the whole time, you've just been asleep to them. When you wake up to your strengths, you wake up to who you are. You see more of yourself and it no longer requires conscious effort. The natural expression of your strengths will unfold.

Consider a moment in your life when you thought you didn't handle the circumstances very well. Look deeply into that moment and consider this – you were expressing your strengths in some form. Your strength was being flexed in some way at the time. You've been looking at that moment with your critical eye thinking, "I could've done that so much better. I didn't handle that very well. I should've..." But you're ignoring your strengths. They were there the whole time. They were being expressed the way you express your strengths, but you were ignoring them.

Believe the following words. When you see where your strengths were standing at that moment, you will undoubtedly connect the dots with several events throughout your life. You will see the thread of truth make its way through your life, and your strengths will go from hugging the wall at the party to standing in the middle of the dance floor with you, empowering you to be who you were meant to be this whole time. You!

The person you've been looking to become, the person you've been looking for this whole time, has been with you throughout your entire life, you've just been ignoring them. See them, feel them, appreciate them, love them. Love who you are. What happens as a result can only be experienced firsthand, not described in words. Go and dance with the dance partner who's been waiting for you this whole time.

"Experience is simply the name we give our mistakes."

OSCAR WILDE

LEARN FROM YOUR MISTAKES

Indecision and its cousin, procrastination, have a very close relative called shame.

Story time! A couple years into my coaching business, I had generated some success for myself and things were working well. Because things were going well for me, I started to believe that it was because of the decisions I was making and I became over-confident in my abilities.

While that's true to some degree, I was taking credit for the portion that wasn't my own doing. Think of a sailor taking credit for the winds that carry his ship across the ocean. He might be a skilled sailor but he's no master of the winds.

This led me to start making decisions with more confidence than I would usually have carried, which came with consequences I had to deal with months later. Consequences that left me bruised with shame and guilt.

It wasn't until hindsight took the reins that I began to see those decisions as mistakes. I started to see those past decisions as choices that weren't beneficial even though at the time I thought they were.

I hadn't gone back in time and changed my decision, just my perception of it as time passed. Because I started to see those decisions as mistakes, I started to develop the habit of being indecisive. I was scared of making another mistake. If that's you, read carefully.

Whenever it came to making any kind of decision, I would procrastinate and sit on the fence. Even with small decisions, like what to eat for dinner, I would wrestle between eating this or that. "Do I want the aftertaste of that to linger after dinner? Oh, I ate Italian two nights ago, I won't have it again tonight." I was becoming silently obsessive over small decisions and it got to a point where I couldn't ignore my behaviour anymore.

In a lot of cases, I would leave the decision-making up to my wife and I would just take a back seat. The responsibility of making decisions for myself became too much. What if I made a mistake again? I'd regret it and have to deal with the consequences. So I stepped away from the responsibility of moving forward in my own life because deciding was just too difficult.

The truth about indecision is that it may seem like you're avoiding making a decision, but you're actually making the decision to not decide. That's a decision in and of itself. Think about it. No matter how many mistakes you make, you can't avoid making decisions in life. You may have fooled yourself into thinking you're avoiding hard decisions but you're not. You're choosing not to choose.

Each day you make decisions that affect how you respond or react to everything that takes place in your life. An example of this is four men I know who were all born the same year. Each of them has lived a very different life. One left his home country as a teenager to build a life in a new land of opportunity. Another was brought to the same country of opportunity by his parents as a young boy. Another man was raised in a rural part of this country, and the fourth spent his youth as a homeless surfer.

They were all born the same year, raised differently and ended up with different outcomes in the later years of their lives. One of them passed away in his fifties, another ended up with a neurodegenerative disease and passed away in his early sixties, another ended up in a business he had begun to resent and wrestled with a number of health conditions, and the fourth, who had started out as a homeless surfer, ended up a multi-millionaire, travelling the world and teaching philosophy.

The stark difference between all of these men – whom I've had personal relationships with – ultimately came down to the decisions they did or didn't make throughout their lives. They all had the same resources and opportunities at their disposal; very little money, a head full of genius, a big heart and a desire to do something meaningful with their lives.

It was an equal playing field for each of them. Some chose to not make decisions, others chose to do something very specific. As each of them moved through life, they inevitably made 'mistakes', but how each person learned and moved on from their 'mistakes' determined the decisions they made in the future. The mistakes they made weren't quite mistakes though.

Here's the mindset part of it. If you're scared of making a mistake in the future it's because there's a memory in your mind of a time where you made a decision that seemed to be a mistake. So moving forward, you make your decisions based on the fear of making the same mistake again. That's no way to truly live. You're avoiding situations in fear of the outcome, but what if by avoiding it, you end up with the outcome you feared?

The way to change your decision-making behaviour is to change how you see your past decisions, particularly your mistakes. Those apparent mistakes drive your choices and indecision moving forward. Changing your perspective on the 'mistakes' you made has a domino effect on your future decisions.

Do this: go back to those memories you have of the 'mistakes' you've made and list out how you and the people you affected had benefitted from your decision back then. Keep listing out the benefits, advantages and upsides of your decision to others and yourself, until you see that it was just as beneficial as it was detrimental. Bring balance and neutrality to the memory.

You can't change what you did or didn't do. That's in the past, but as long as you see it as a mistake, you'll use all your present energy to attempt to change something you can't touch. By changing your perception of your memory – the only thing you can control – you will most definitely alter your present and future.

If you perceive you've made a financial mistake – something that cost you a lot of money – do the same exercise as above, list out all of the benefits you gained from the expense and write down the monetary value you received next to each lesson. Keep doing this until the value you received equals the amount of money you thought you lost in your 'mistake'.

To take it a step further, ask yourself, "If you had to pay to learn the same lesson somewhere else, would you have paid more?" Sometimes we have to be put through certain experiences to learn certain lessons. This is my definition of the university of life. You have been gifted lessons that no one can take away from you. To trust that subtle inner-knowing.

I had believed that I was going to move through my life making fewer mistakes than the average person because I was able to learn life lessons from watching other people's mistakes as much as going through my own experiences. I quickly learned that no one is devoid of making mistakes. In fact, it's been my mistakes and failures in life that have given me the knowledge, trust and wisdom to follow my heart more consistently.

This book exists undoubtedly because of a tonne of 'mistakes' I have made. Those men I mentioned earlier had all made mistakes. The shame and guilt they chose to carry most definitely impacted how they lived out their lives. One trapped himself in his own business only to be riddled with bouts of anxiety and panic. Another trapped himself in his body, too scared to be himself and love himself for who he is. Another trapped himself in a job that kept him away from his home and his loved ones. Yet another did what he could – including the exercise I mentioned – to drop the anchors of shame and guilt so he could see himself as worthy of fulfilling the dream and vision he had. I'll leave you to work out whose life matches with which story.

At some point your shame and guilt will exhaust you to the point of drowning. It doesn't have to though. You can choose to change your shame and guilt. You can change how you see yourself.

Instead of carrying around the unnecessary burden of seeing your past as a collection of mistakes and bad decisions, change your perception of the past. Turn your mistakes into your badges of honour, your certificate of experience. Appreciate them as a part of your journey through the university of life. Doing that is certainly no mistake.

"The word 'happy' would lose its meaning if it were not balanced by sadness."

CARL G. JUNG

SHAKE OFF YOUR SADNESS AND DEPRESSION

Expectations are a bittersweet thing. They're a tool that can make or break your spirit. They can lead you to incredible highs and drown you in lows that have no bottom. Either way expectations exist because they are necessary, but are they being used in the wisest way? Maybe not.

We've all got expectations and they vary depending on what we want from life, family, friends, work and the world. But how useful are they? Personally, they've helped me achieve some goals that I never thought I'd be capable of achieving, but on the other hand, expectations are what led me down into four long, dark years of depression in my early twenties.

I spent the earlier part of my life believing that I was destined for achieving something great, something much bigger than me, and I was going to be wildly successful at it. But what ended up happening was not what I expected. Not at all.

It was around my twentieth birthday and I was reflecting on the way I was living my life and then looking at the dreams I had for myself. What I found was that both were very distant from each other, not even remotely close. So I did what I had always done – I asked why. "Why had nothing happened the way that I had imagined?" I continued to ask myself until the answer reared its face. The answer floored me and initiated the downward spiral into depression that spanned four years of my life. The answer to my question was that I had done nothing towards realising my dreams. Nothing!

Throughout the four years that I was wrestling with my beliefs, my feelings of self-defeat and questioning why I was bothering to wake up in the morning, I came to realise something that was crucial to climbing out of the depression. I realised that it wasn't the lack of actions that was the problem, it was the expectation I had placed on myself. I believed, for a number of different reasons, that as long as I dreamed I was going to be a great contributor to the world, that it would eventually happen by pure fate, destiny and divine intervention. Man, was I wrong.

Think about it. If you're stuck in a desert and in dying need of water, you're not going to stand still and hinge your future survival on the possibility that rain will come to you. You'll do what you can to find water, dig wells, look for an oasis, follow animals or truck water in. You won't stop until you find water. Not only was I expecting the rain to come to me, I wasn't even willing to do a rain dance.

So what did I do to change my depression? I asked myself, "Is this life that I'm dreaming about the life that I truly want for myself, or have I somehow taken everybody else's interpretation of the perfect life and decided that I want that version?" In truth, it wasn't the life that I wanted. It was a concoction of many different lives.

So I changed my expectation. I persistently asked myself what I truly wanted and slowly started working towards that. The interesting thing about it was that working towards the life that I truly wanted took no conscious effort. I just did it, no questions asked. Like water seeking its own level – it doesn't need to try to, it just moves in its natural direction, seeking the place where it belongs.

Think of a cinema screen with twenty projectors each projecting different movies. How are you supposed to see anything clearly? The picture would be so noisy that you wouldn't know what you're watching. If your expectations of life, your beliefs of who you are and what you truly want, are an idea of everyone else's desires, then you're going to struggle to see your movie on the big screen.

These days? I'm closer to living the life that I truly want for myself and I get to show people how to achieve the same for themselves. These words are an example of that. It's my version of what I wanted. A book with insights for you from the people who taught me.

If you're depressed or frustrated with yourself, the world, or anyone in your life, look at what you're expecting. Is what you're expecting realistic and is it truly what you want, or are you just taking someone else's expectations and making them

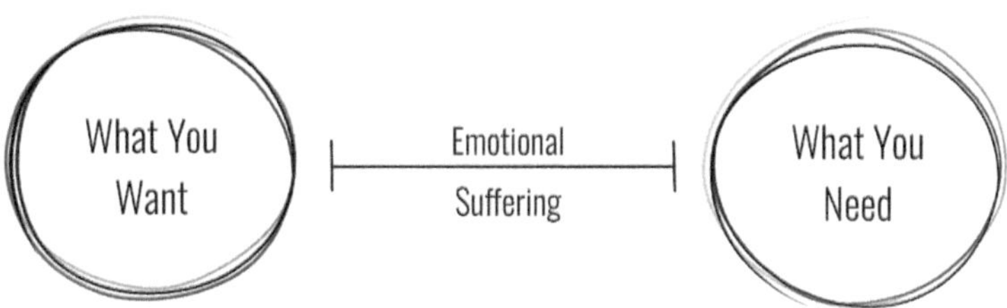

your own? Are you being a contortionist, conforming yourself to the world?

Depression doesn't mean you need to be changed. You're not broken or needing to be fixed. The problem is that your expectations don't match who you are. Align your expectations with who you truly are and the person you awaken to will prove to be remarkable. Your intuition – inner knowing – is trying to wake you up to this.

Simply put, when you're depressed, change your expectation to one that is real – not some fantasy – and the depression will alleviate. Depression isn't as complicated as you may think. Your depression is your intuition doing what it can for you to wake up to your expectations of yourself and the world.

It's the whispers you're not listening to that require more obvious forms of communication for you to hear. The more you ignore them, the greater the depression. I dare say that taking an anti-depressant is like covering up the 'check engine' light on your car. Or similar to when you experience physical pain. You wouldn't want to cover it up and hope the cause goes away magically. There's something important that could use your attention. Don't ignore it. If feeling depressed is going to get your attention, then it's serving its purpose.

So it's time to wake up. Listen to your intuition. The world is waiting for you to share what you have inside.

You are worthy of your depression. That's because your depression is fighting to get you onto your path. It's doing whatever it can to show you that you are not honouring who you are. That means who you truly are is worth fighting for, even if that means using depression to keep the fight going.

This gives the suffering of depression a deeper meaning than you initially believed. To be experiencing the depression you're dealing with means you're worth fighting for. Time to recognise that and to realise you've been exactly who you're meant to be this whole time.

P.S. It would be wise for me to make a comment on prescribed medication for treating depression. Medication has its place for the treatment of emotional challenges. For example, if you don't have the framework to navigate your psychology and mindset and medication keeps your chin above water in the short term, then it's helpful, so long as the underlying emotional cause is being addressed and worked through.

If you're taking anti-depressants or anti-anxiety medication, the last thing I want you to do is throw it into the rubbish and go through the motions of coming off the medication cold turkey. My suggestion is to do so with the help of your prescribing doctor or a professional who has experience helping people come off of medication. If your doctor isn't willing to help you do so to any degree then find a doctor who will. Don't be reckless but also don't assume that medication is the only way. No one wants to feel dependent on medication to feel a degree of normalcy (whatever that means). You're allowed to want to come off your medication.

"Courage is the mastery of fear, not the absence of fear."

MARK TWAIN

MAKE FEAR YOUR FRIEND

Fear is a fascinating thing. It's not tangible, it doesn't have an audible voice and certainly can't physically manipulate anything. Yet it has the ability to control even the most powerful people in the world. It can drive you to make irrational, dangerous and 'out-of-character' decisions without whispering a word. It can command control over your body and impact the actions you take or don't take.

Here is this thing that has such an effect on collective humanity and on an individual level yet the vast majority of its victims don't understand it. It's a mythological wildebeest that lives in the shadows of people's minds and has developed an air of mystery around its purpose and its motives for showing up.

The thing is, once understood, it can go from an untameable beast to a domesticated house pet that will be a loyal friend throughout your life. Notice how I didn't mention anything about slaying it or ridding yourself of it? That's because it's impossible to rid yourself of fear. No one in the realm of human existence has been completely fearless. Even if their biographies paint a fearless story.

Fear has a place in this world, otherwise, it wouldn't exist. It's here to help you. Once you come to understand the language it uses, becoming friends with fear will be easier.

Let's start with how fear is influenced by time. In the simplified diagram below you'll see time as a linear thing – a straight line. In the centre is this present moment, to the left is the past and to the right is the future.

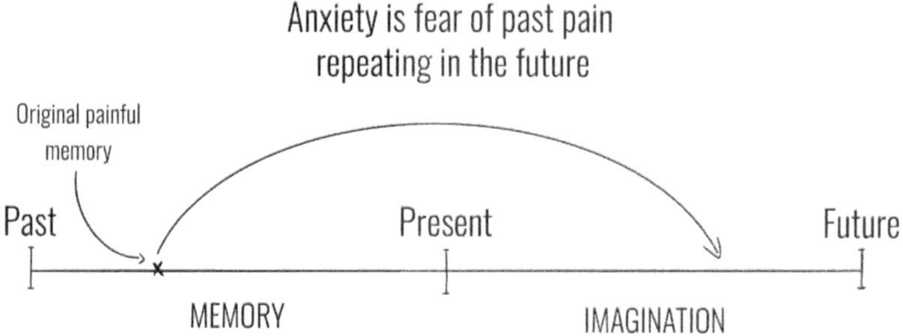

Your future pain is driven by memory of past pain repeating itself. If you dissolve the memory, then fear of future will be gone.

When fear arises in your mind, it happens because you're worrying about something in the future happening to you. For example, you have a flight coming up and you're worried you're going to miss your flight which will, in your perception, leave you stranded. This story you're worrying about is all taking place in the future of this moment. You're imagining a future pain – being stranded.

However, the truth is, you can't have an imagination about something without having a memory of it somewhere in your past. Balance exists in linear time too. Your imagination balances out your memory and vice versa. So if you have a fear of something happening in the future, it's because you have a memory of it taking place in the past. (For more on that, read the chapter on how we form beliefs (page 23).)

This also means that you can't fear the unknown. This is something a lot of people say. They believe they have a fear of the unknown. But how can you fear something you don't know? This idea gets spread without knowledge of what I explained above. You don't fear the unknown. You picture a scene, like a movie, in your mind and that triggers the fear. You're imagining something happening – it's just being labelled as 'unknown'. You're actually picturing the past repeating itself.

The most effective way I have seen and experienced for dissolving the fears of the future is to dissolve the pain of the past.

Consider driving a car. Having the accelerator pushed to the floor will drive the car forward. If you press the brake while the accelerator is still engaged, the car will slow down and eventually come to a stop. But the moment you take your foot off the brake again, the car will speed forward. It seems ridiculous to stop a car this way. The sensible way would be to disengage the accelerator and then use the brakes, alternating between the two pedals depending on how far you want to move forward and stop. This makes coming to a complete stop smoother and faster.

When it comes to dealing with fear, most people hit the brakes as hard as they can while the accelerator is still engaged.

However, the moment they take their foot off the brake for a rest, the fear has a good handle on the accelerator and drives you forward into situations which are harder to manage.

By dissolving your past pain you're taking fear's foot off the accelerator and putting yourself back in control. This stops the pain from driving your fear forward.

Here's how to do that. When you're worried, concerned or fearful about something happening in the future, for example, being humiliated, think back to a time in the past when you were humiliated. Take yourself back there and revisit the humiliation you experienced. If you feel any resistance or discomfort then you're on the right path. Don't fight the feeling, go back into the memory and re-experience it. Once you're in that memory, ask yourself how being humiliated – or whatever the negative experience – helped you at the time.

Look for the benefits, gains and advantages that you received from that experience. Every positive has a negative and every negative, a positive. Look for what you received. Did people sympathise and give you attention? Did you develop a relationship with someone as a result? Did you get a new opportunity as a result? Did you earn extra income? Did you get some personal space? Did you learn something new about yourself? Did you gain some clarity about your path in life? Look at the various ways in which you gained benefits from this experience until you see it in a balanced way. This is called equilibrium or neutrality. The zero-point between a positive and negative charge.

The reason you fear the past happening again is that you can't see how the triggering event helped you in the past. You believe, moving forward, that you're a victim of challenges, difficulties and one-sided events. The truth is you're not, it's just your perception. I'll reiterate my point. Life is filled with opposites. Good, bad, light, dark, positive and negative. They need each other to exist.

Having only positive electricity does not complete the circuit and certainly doesn't turn the lights on. You need negative to complete the circuit to allow the electrons to flow and for electricity to flow. Positive and negative are inseparable. They exist together, for each other, which means they walk hand-in-hand throughout life.

So your apparent negative experience had positives packed away in that same moment. It just requires your awareness and your investigative eye. Use your natural ability to see both sides to help you uncover the hidden potential in those seemingly negative and painful experiences of your past. Do this to bring your understanding back into equilibrium and neutrality. You owe yourself a balanced perspective. This will make it very difficult for your fear to live in your house of balance. It's akin to a fresh breeze of clean air and sunlight filtering through what was once a dark and dusty home – your mind.

If you're doing this and not seeing that it's balanced, list out more benefits that you received from your experience. Write out as many as you need – it may even be fifty – to help you get to a balanced state. Don't stop until you feel the shift inside and you open up to a sense of gratitude for what had happened. Gratitude is the goal here because you can't fear what you're grateful for.

The problem with fear is that we're taught to overcome it. We're not taught to see that fear is helping us. It's feedback that there's something about yourself you haven't yet honoured. There's something in your mind that is blocking you from seeing the whole picture. The fear is your inner knowing subtly suggesting that it's wise for you to open up to what you're not fully conscious of. You're stuck in this semi-sleeping state and you're having a nightmare about how things are going to be emotionally or physically painful. Your inner knowing is standing over you, trying to wake you up and show you that it's just a dream. You're convinced the pain and fear are real, but when you wake up, you'll come to realise it was only half the story.

The whole story is that your challenges and adversities are helping you discover an untapped potential that lies within you. What would you have missed out on if these challenges hadn't occurred in your life? Would you be the person you are today? Not the person riddled with fear and anxiety, but the person who had the inner strength to survive anyway.

Next time fear shows up at your doorstep, welcome it in, turn the kettle on and ask it what lesson it has for you today. No doubt it will be a valuable one.

"It is not events that disturb people, it is their judgments concerning them."

EPICTETUS

APPRECIATE ANXIETY

Here is a beast that many have attempted to slay but instead ended up being held captive to it. Anxiety is an elusive thing that cannot be touched, grappled with or killed, and yet it has the power to bring anyone to complete emotional vulnerability. It's a state of mind that can shift the calmest of people into a spiral of impending doom, tension and loneliness, which can make normal functioning difficult.

When anxiety and panic take hold, it can feel like you're lying in a jumping castle while people are jumping all around you. You're being thrown around and have no control over it. And to make things worse, the more you try to get a grip, the stronger the loss of control feels.

My attempt here is to cover the various facets of anxiety that you may come to experience. If you'd like to know more about what to do when someone you care about is experiencing anxiety and panic (that is, if you haven't experienced it before), read chapter titled "Control The Panic" (page 201).

Also, I want to point out that my approach here is to address the psychological and emotional aspect of anxiety. There are other factors that can affect or trigger anxiety in people that are not just psychological or emotional. More on that later.

For now, let's get into the dirty details of what anxiety is to better understand the elusive devil that it is. Anxiety is defined by the Oxford dictionary as "a feeling of worry, nervousness, or unease about something with an uncertain outcome." That's exactly it, it's something that is imagined in the future. Something that seems to be uncertain or unknown. It is similar to fear but has a subtle difference to fear, in that an experience of fear is something you believe to be present in this moment.

Anxiety, on the other hand, is something imagined in the future. The fundamental difference between fear and anxiety is simply now versus then. (Read more on the details of fear in the chapter on understanding fear (page 95).)

Anxiety is considered a normal response to events when you're lacking enough information to make an educated assessment of the situation. Chronic anxiety is where it starts to get messy. When your anxiety starts to determine your decisions and actions, it's interfering with your life and potentially getting in the way of you achieving what you once thought was important. This happens because there's an underlying cause that is doing a fantastic job of hiding in plain sight.

I've mentioned before how good the past is at effecting our future. It can be the thing that determines *how* we move through our lives. Experiences in the past can shape our beliefs and add new details to our rule book on life, even if those details are only half-truths.

Psychologically speaking, the underlying cause of your anxiety is something that you have experienced in your past. Meaning, you've been through it before. The sense of doom that you're envisioning is one that you feel you've had to deal with before. You've had an experience before and you're anticipating the same thing happening again. So you've positioned your mind into a fight/flight/freeze response. All or nothing. That right there has the power to instil panic in anyone. That right there is a normal response to a threat, whether it's imagined or real. The tripwire that gets you falling into the pit of anxiety and panic are the lopsided thoughts, memories and beliefs that you have about your past experiences.

So how do you stop yourself from walking into the tripwire in the first place? Like most things in this book, the place I start with is the question "Why?". Why might you be experiencing anxiety? Why would that happen even though it feels like it has no value or purpose?

Well, what if I told you that it does have value and it does have a purpose? I know, at first this sounds ridiculous but, like I asked in the chapter on balance, why would something exist if it served no inherent purpose? Why would something continue to exist if it provided no value? So using that framework of thinking, wouldn't something as seemingly cruel as anxiety have a purpose that is serving you in some way? Maybe.

What if it was serving as feedback? What if the anxiety was an inbuilt imbalance detector telling you that something was up and it would be best to address it? What if it was your intuition's way of telling you that trying to live through anxiety isn't enough?

Living with anxiety is like snapping the stem off the weeds instead of digging down into the soil and removing the roots that the weed is growing from. Cutting the weed back to the surface of the soil only removes it from sight. It will grow back. Removing the root helps you see where it all started. Pouring weed killer over it can work too, just like taking chemical neurotransmitter disruptors, but that doesn't educate you on why it was there in the first place. It makes you dependent on using weed killer instead of working out a strategy for minimising the weed. I think you get my point here.

Your anxiety is a post-it note in your mind trying to get your attention. It's saying, "Your view is limited. You're seeing only half of the picture and you'd get a lot of value from looking again." But what is it that you're not seeing? Let's go looking.

You experience anxiety because you're imagining something in the future causing you some sense of impending doom. You believe something will be the end of you. Why would you believe that to be true? Because there was a time in your past when you experienced something similar that went 'bad'. You expected things to go a certain way, and they didn't, they turned around and did a complete 180° flip. So now, instead of expecting things to go according to plan, you're anticipating what happened back then and that's making you anxious.

Here's an extreme example. I'll use sailing because I like the ocean. You set sail on a half-day adventure north to a beautiful coastal town that you used to visit when you were a kid. On your way up you sail into a storm just off the coast and it batters your boat, makes you ill and throws your loved one overboard, while you spend a frantic fifteen minutes doing everything you can to bring them back aboard. What should've been a four-hour venture turns into seven hours that really feels like two days. After your stay in the coastal town, you get set to sail home and as you do, the wind picks up stronger than expected and you immediately think of the storm you endured on your way there. You instantly begin to anticipate the storm you experienced days before and the pain you endured. This triggers a sense of anxiety, and worry starts to take hold. You know what follows.

Moving forward, anytime the winds pick up strength and you're away from home, you anticipate getting stuck or stranded and not knowing if you're going to make it to safety. So each day you head out, even if it's just to pick up some groceries, you find yourself checking the detailed weather forecast, planning all available routes home and making sure you don't go anywhere you might get trapped or stranded.

Before the first storm, you didn't behave in this anxious manner. You would just head out, get stuff done, navigate your day and head home when you were ready.

One moment gave you enough of an experience to shock you into forming a belief that would determine the way you live the rest of your life. A defining moment you might say.

Anxiety is an effect or a symptom. It has a beginning. It has a cause. It presents itself for a reason. It's telling you that something is missing from your awareness that has the potential to completely shift the way you see yourself, other people and the event, whatever it is.

It's important for you to remember the value of a balanced perception here. Your experiences are equally both good and bad, filled with pain and pleasure, a source of challenge and support, both positive and negative. That is the truth of it. How you view the experience, what you focus on, determines what you see.

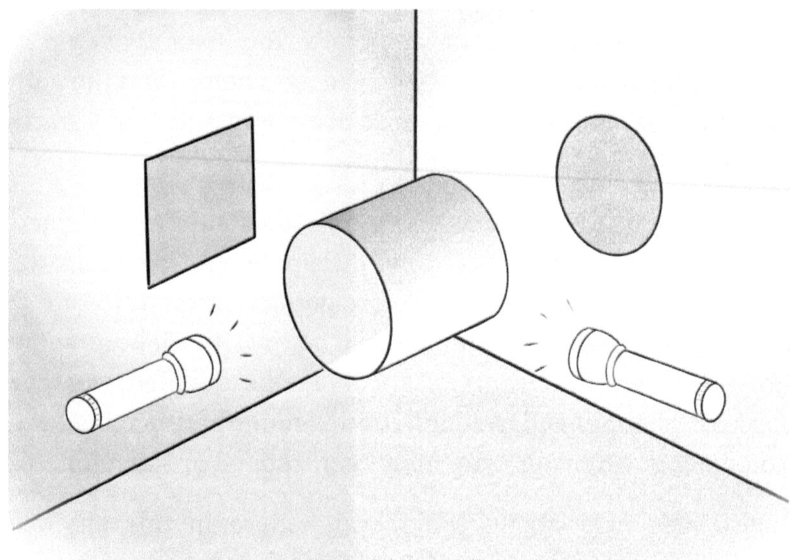

Depending on your position and your perspective, you will see a different image. Perspective is important, because if where you were standing determined what you saw, then where you move to could change what you see.

I'm not talking about physically moving, but about moving the things you see in your memories. Like I've said, your memories of your past are driving the imaginations of your future. By re-exploring your memories and changing what you saw, you get the chance to change what you see moving forward. Sounds simple, and it is, but it has the power to change what you think is possible.

A common experience for people who deal with anxiety is that just before they experience the sense of anxiety, they perceive being trapped in some way. They perceive they are being cornered, trapped or confined by something or someone. The important thing to note here is that it can be a real or imagined trap. Whether it's real or imagined, it triggers the same response in the body and the mind. Your subconscious cannot tell the difference between imagination and reality. So even if it's imagined pain, your mind will tell your body to respond accordingly. Just like the audience believes the magician made the queen of hearts magically disappear from the deck. It's a convincing illusion until proven otherwise.

So let's go behind the curtain of the illusion and find out what's really happening. For those of you who are dogmatic about your beliefs on psychology, genetic neurochemical imbalances or the spiels of some supposed expert, put the book down. You're probably not ready for the following words. That's okay, you can come back when you are. For those of you ready to continue, keep your mind open. Some of what I have to say may seem obvious and other things might leave you speechless. That's what happened to me.

Let's explore your anxiety. Think of a time you had an anxiety attack. You'll most likely find that there was a trigger hiding somewhere in the moment just before you felt yourself get swept away. Someone may have said something, something may have happened and then you thought to yourself *that was overwhelming,* and then the anxiety started to surface. The question is, what happened or what was said?

Then, you'll want to ask, what was challenging about what happened? Just because something happened doesn't automatically mean you'll dislike it. There's a specific reason you felt challenged. There's a particular way you're perceiving the event and that is what's causing your reaction.

In terms of the balancing scale I've mentioned before (read the chapter on balance (page 39)), you were seeing more bad than good in whatever you perceived in the moments before you experienced the anxiety.

There is something you're seeing that's only half of the picture which is triggering the sense of being trapped. Your perception is what's trapping you. I know that seems easy for me to write, but I don't write this lightly. I say it from much of my own experience with anxiety and just as much experience with the people I've worked with over the years.

Your perception of that moment just before your anxiety surfaced is what's holding the anxiety in place. Moving forward, whenever you experience an event that has some similarity to the first memory, your mind will jump to the same thought, believe the same pain will occur and therefore, you'll get anxious and panicked about the same thing repeating itself. Each time this happens, you add and compound new layers of detail to the memory, making it easier to be triggered.

The more details that get compounded, the harder it is for you to immediately see the original cause. Your vision of the original event becomes blocked by the fog of all the other triggers that are linked. It doesn't become impossible to identify the original memory, it's just harder to get there without someone guiding you.

Here's an example of a woman I worked with years ago. Catherine lived in a rural part of Australia, about a 90-minute drive out from the closest major city. She was in her late forties when we started working together, and she was dealing with very strong waves of anxiety and panic. She, like most people dealing with anxiety, was covering it up and hiding it from others. In fact, she ran and owned her own business which required she spend a lot of time driving around from client to client. She had plans to expand her business to another regional area but struggled driving longer than thirty minutes away from home, especially if she was by herself.

Through our conversation, I uncovered some heavy anchors that she was carrying from her days as a paramedic. Working together, we managed to shift that memory from one of shame to one of gratitude. Even though she had managed to shift this traumatic event, she still struggled with her anxiety around travelling by herself.

So I asked her for more details about what specifically made her anxious about travelling long distances. I wanted to know what she imagined would happen and what she feared was going to unfold. Her answers shed a lot of light on her dilemma and as soon as I pointed out that her anxiety about what might happen in the future was based on a similar situation that happened in the past, she immediately knew what the cause was. The memory of where it started came to her in a flash.

She said to me that she worried about getting lost and getting stranded somewhere unfamiliar. She was worried about being stuck far away from towns or anyone she knew and feared not having an escape from the situation, leaving her with a sense of being trapped. Being in an unfamiliar environment overwhelmed her and led her to feel like she wasn't in control.

With anxiety and panic, the sense of having no control and feeling trapped go hand in hand.

Here's the most overlooked part of anxiety. Because Catherine was so overwhelmed with the sensation of being trapped and out of control, she wasn't able to bring her attention to anything else. This adds fuel to the fire and exacerbates the experience. She was only seeing half of the picture. What she didn't realise was where she was in control, and where she possessed freedom in those moments. These were qualities of the other half of the balancing scale.

The opposite of being trapped is having freedom, and the opposite of losing control is having control. Both sides exist together. They're two sides of the same coin just like positive and negative. But if all you're doing is focussing on one side, you'll never see the side that was there the whole time, which is also the side that will bring your anxiety to rest.

You might be wondering, 'how could seeing the opposing force to anxiety and panic help calm the mind and body?' It happens by bringing your mind back to its centre. It brings your mind back to the space between the two extremes of the emotional state. That space in between, right in the middle of the two sides, is where the underlying purpose and meaning of the experience exists. This is the place your mind naturally wants to come to. Polarised emotions will prevent your mind from getting back to this natural place of balance or emotional homeostasis.

How many times have you experienced something traumatic or incredibly difficult and asked yourself, "Why is this happening?" and struggled to come up with an answer? That's because you're still stuck on one side of the scale. If you truly want to know why it's happening or has happened, if you want to know the hidden meaning and purpose of the experience, you must navigate to the half-way point between the pain and the pleasure, the positive and negative, to then reveal the truth of what was happening beneath the surface of reality.

When Catherine opened up and told me the details of what was making her anxious, she was able to reveal to me that she had a memory of feeling stranded and trapped on a bus that was taking her three hours into the country away from her home. She was visiting a boyfriend and used the bus to get there. The bus stopped at a town about halfway along the journey and when she took the time to look around, she realised she had no idea where she was, how far from home or her destination she was and how she would get home. It was dusk and there was still some time before she expected to arrive. The only other people on the bus were one other passenger and the bus driver, who she was sitting right behind. Keep in mind, this was decades before the internet, smartphones and GPS technology for consumers.

Once she became aware of the fact that she was in an unfamiliar environment and didn't know where her home was, she panicked. Anxiety started as a ball in her stomach and washed over her like a wave of tension and adrenaline. At that point, she was completely blind to where she was in control and how she was actually free. Tunnel vision kicked in and made it hard to see anything but what she feared. So we went digging and as we did, she realised that she had the freedom to step off the bus at the bus stop and the opportunity to turn herself in any direction she wanted. She also realised that she had full control over her body, she could dictate where her feet would take her, the words her mouth would express and the thoughts and beliefs she carried.

What came next was remarkable. She struck up a conversation with the bus driver, asking him about the area, the route and what else he knew. She didn't appreciate it until our conversation but she was controlling herself by engaging in a conversation to get as much information as she could about the area.

Catherine thought she was just distracting herself from the anxiety as best she could. She was in more control than she was able to admit at the time and when she saw that she was equally in control and out of control in that moment, she saw something very different to an anxiety-riddled woman. She saw a resourceful and intellectual woman making the most of the situation she was in. By placing herself in the gap between the two extremes of having control and losing control, Catherine was able to see herself for who she truly is, therefore dropping the anxiety and fear in that moment and in the future.

By the end of the conversation, Catherine went from being consumed by fear about driving into rural towns alone to enthusiastic about doing it alone. She went from being panicked about getting on a plane for a one-hour flight – it felt like a similar trapping environment to the bus – to wanting to do it and make an adventure of it.

Your anxieties about the future are not random. They're specific to what you've experienced and what you haven't been able to see the complete picture of. You've fallen for the illusion of half of the picture at the time of intense anxiety and so whenever the smoke and mirrors appear again, you immediately believe what you see.

You're not to blame for seeing things that way and you're certainly not worthy of carrying around any shame about it. You were having a normal reaction to what seemed like a distressing situation. But that's just it. When you look more closely at what happened you discover that things aren't quite what they originally seemed.

Remember this, if you experience anxiety or panic about something, it's your intuition putting a post-it note front and centre for you to read. It's telling you that there's something in your past you haven't yet appreciated about yourself. It's the check engine warning light on an imbalanced memory. There is an experience you had that you haven't yet come to appreciate. So take the time to reflect. Go back and reassess what you believed to be true. Find the gap between the two sides and you'll see something that is truly remarkable. You were being shown who you truly are capable of being and that's a lesson that can never be taken away from you.

A note on biochemistry and its effect on anxiety. It's been disputed for decades that anxiety comes from a chemical imbalance in the brain which can be corrected with medication. This is when medication is used to fill in the gaps of the neurochemical holes. Medicine has made leaps and bounds in assisting people with biochemical imbalances. However, the pitfall, as I see it, is that it's used as a bandaid and overlooks the cause of anxiety in the first place. Do biochemical imbalances cause anxiety or does anxiety trigger biochemical imbalances? Will we ever truly know the answer to that question? It's a chicken and egg argument that leaves people even more confused about how to address the anxiety. There is no doubt that nutrition, the microbiome and the enteric brain in the gut are all impacted and have an effect on people's experience of anxiety and other mental conditions. Use medication and chemical assistance if it's been prescribed by someone who understands the details of your situation, but please, do not blatantly accept the notion that you are broken and this is the only way for you to live your life. It's not. Use all of what works to help you work through your anxiety and all of its triggers. If that means using a combination of medication and nutritional supplementation with therapeutic techniques, then do that. You have more power than others – particularly professionals – will have you believe. Know that your anxiety is feedback and that while you use chemical assistance, you can very well get to the root of the origin of your anxiety. Oh, and I'm not a doctor or medical professional, so take my note on neurochemical imbalances with as much salt as you like if you must. There, my lawyer's anxiety has been addressed too.

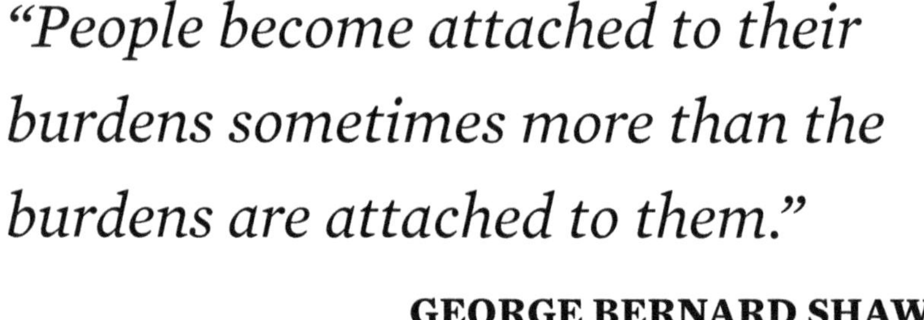

"People become attached to their burdens sometimes more than the burdens are attached to them."

GEORGE BERNARD SHAW

END THE GUILT TRIP

Here's an anchor, or rather an anvil, tied to your ankle. Chances are you've spent most of your life finding a way to live with it. You've been hobbling along thinking that it's normal to move and function this way. What doesn't help is as you look around at friends, family and colleagues, you see that everyone is trying to make their way around this world with the same heavy weight tied to their ankle. So, yeah, you're going to believe this way of living is normal. You're wrong.

Did you know that the word for guilt in Dutch is the same word used for debt? Let the Dutch teach you something about what's happening psychologically when you experience guilt. The more guilt you experience, the greater the debt you lump yourself with. Notice how I said that you lump yourself. That was intentional.

Let's get to the juicy part by starting with what guilt is. It's simply when you've done something to someone else that you believe was bad, negative, a hindrance, problematic or painful for them. Basically, if you cause someone pain you feel guilty. The greater the pain that you perceive you caused, the greater the guilt you experience. Easy to follow, right?

Well, then what about the infamous guilt-trips that you get from that person who always manages to make you feel guilty about doing something? You know who I'm talking about. You say you've got plans, you're going to go do something or you want to do something for yourself and you get something like, "Oh, no problem. I'll just go and do this by myself. I'm used to it anyway." That has an undertone of sarcasm.

How good is that line? It's made the strongest of people crumble at the knees – yes, I picked the knees for a reason.

Anyway, the reason you're so susceptible to their guilt-trips is that you already feel guilty, they're just serving it up on a silver platter and choosing to reveal it to you from under a cloche. Voila! Your well-cooked guilt, madame. Watch out for the aftertaste. You might like to wash it down with our finest bottle of passive aggression from 2003. Bon appétit!

You know those times you've experienced someone's guilt-trip and it hasn't worked on you? That's because you didn't believe that what you did was bad and guilt-worthy. So you don't order the guilt and get to skip through to dessert.

How do you shake this guilt when it does crop up? Well, change how you see the pain that you caused. By changing how you see an obstacle, it stops causing you pain. Well, you feel guilty because you perceive that your actions or words have placed an obstacle in front of someone you care about. More so, you believe that the obstacle is causing them some degree of pain. In other words, the greater the pain that you perceive you caused someone, the greater the guilt you experience. You pile on the guilt to compensate for the pain you caused. Think of it like causing yourself pain to make yourself feel better about the pain you caused them.

Now, think about this: If you can change how you see an obstacle that's been placed in your own path, then you can change the way you see an obstacle you placed in the path of another traveller.

You do this by looking for all the different ways the obstacle is actually helping your 'victim'.

Let's look at bullying as a prime example since I experienced a lot of it throughout my youth. My bullies didn't feel guilty for their actions. They did the deed and moved on. They even felt good for it afterwards. Why? Because I wasn't someone they looked up to, admired or valued. They saw me as beneath them. On the other hand, if they had done the exact same thing to someone they valued or admired, they would feel incredible degrees of guilt. Same actions, different perception. No amount of guilt-tripping would have made them feel 'bad' for what they did to me because they didn't feel the guilt to begin with. Little do they know, they are part of the reason I'm writing this book today, so even if they did feel guilty, it's unwarranted.

Back to my point. You can choose how you see your actions. By listing out all of the ways you actually helped that person through your pain-causing actions, you begin to liberate yourself from the shackle you clasped on your ankle. Change your perception. Change the associations you've made with your actions and it'll be harder for you to see what you did as the pain-inducing behaviour you've labelled it as.

The truth about guilt is that it's actually a selfish emotion. It's really selfish for you to experience guilt. Reread that. By letting yourself slump into the emotion of guilt for an extended period of time, you allow yourself to focus so much on how you feel that you're unable to see how you were actually helping the person at the other end of your behaviour. You'd rather focus on your feelings than on how you're helping people. Selfish

I also want to note here what my mentor suggested to me years ago. He said that "Guilt is a big source of altruistic behaviour." Why? Remember the Dutch word for guilt? That's why. It's the psychological debt that you're carrying around with you. Whenever you're doing something altruistic you're attempting to pay off the debt in your mind. So much so that if you inspect the details of your altruistic behaviour, you'll discover that the person on the receiving end of your altruism has some kind of similar characteristic to the person you feel you owe it to.

For example, I had a client who was late to pay me each month for no other reason than because he kept forgetting to and found other things to do with the money. So when I reminded him, he'd tell me how sorry he was and then he'd forget again. Usually, I would say, "Please pay before our next session because I don't get my time and energy back once it's been given to you." Except I didn't confront him and say this because I saw parts of myself in him from when I was younger. I saw the kid who didn't know how to manage money, who spent it on stuff that wasn't profitable and felt bad about putting him in an uncomfortable – tight – place with his money. So I let him off the hook several times because of the guilt I felt towards him – the past me.

What I couldn't see was that if I put him on the financial ropes and set boundaries for myself and respected his money, I could very well prevent him from doing the same with larger amounts of money and less forgiving people if the habit continued into the future. I didn't confront him because of my guilt. I was too caught up in feeling bad for him to help him. This is me being selfish because I was trying to rescue the younger me by helping him.

Pick a situation that has left you feeling guilty in some way and you'll find that you're experiencing pity rather than seeing yourself as a helping hand. Altruism can very well be a hindrance. Help them by helping yourself. You can't help others see your actions as beneficial if you don't first.

Consider turning someone down or leaving them behind as an example. By leaving them to be by themselves, to be alone or to be lonely, you're helping them confront something they may be running from. Helping them stand up to and confront whatever they're experiencing. Is it that their actions have pushed people away? Is it that they're scared to be alone with their thoughts for a long period of time? Have they been putting off studying or calling someone? Maybe it's something as simple as they're too scared to make themselves a priority and to do something for themselves. When you leave them alone, they don't have an excuse. They'll go and do something, find something that nourishes their soul. They can spend time doing something that inspires them and wakes up the calling inside to do something bigger with their lives.

You get my point. Just because you're leaving someone alone doesn't mean you're doing something worthy of guilt. People benefit from their obstacles even if they've been placed there by you. These obstacles that you create for others can cause people pain but that pain serves a purpose. It helps them. As long as you hold onto the belief that the pain you're causing them is only bad for them without any good, you'll shackle yourself with guilt. You're buying into your own lopsided perception.

This guilt will without a doubt drive you to make decisions that leave you in a debt of some form. That debt usually shows its face in the financial form but isn't limited to it, like I mentioned earlier.

Allow me to make a quick note on the financial debt you're currently dealing with. Let's assume it's not the kind of spending that's intended to fill a void of purpose and meaning in your life. Have you considered what you've been spending your money on that has put you in a position of debt? Have you bought things for others out of guilt? Have you overspent on something you originally planned to spend less on because you felt guilty about how low the original price was?

There's a common joke about how men spend money on expensive things like cars and houses and jewellery to compensate for the size of their genitals. Outside of trying to fill a void, you're probably spending a lot of your money out of guilt without realising it. Something to think about. That's it for the topic of money in this chapter.

To release yourself from the shackles of guilt you've been carrying, consider doing this exercise. List out all the ways that your actions which you feel guilty about had helped the person you 'hurt'. Keep listing answers until you feel the shift. You'll know when the guilt drops because you won't feel the need to beat yourself up for your behaviour. You'll just get it. You'll understand why it happened and how it actually worked out for everyone affected. Yes, I've done this with extreme cases too. It works no matter what it is you feel guilty about.

This does not mean that you can go and deliberately cause trouble for others and then dissolve the guilt. This isn't a free ticket to be reckless without consequences. All actions and decisions have consequences or effects. The intention here is to help alleviate you of the unwarranted guilt that you've been carrying around.

Holding on to feeling guilty is only serving you and your pity party. Focussing on this feeling gives you an excuse to distract yourself from something deeper and more worthy of your attention. Not anymore. You can't unread what you've just read. You can't hold onto your guilt now. I've just handed the keys to the shackles you've been hobbling around in for years. Time for you to take them off. It'll help you get further than you imagined. Take it from someone who felt responsible for the suffering and death of loved ones. If I had allowed it to, the guilt would have crushed these words before they reached the page, let alone making it into your hands. That's what guilt can do to self-worth and the ability to share what's deep inside. Free yourself of these shackles, you deserve it.

"The trouble with most of us is that we would rather be ruined by praise than saved by criticism."

NORMAN VINCENT PEALE

LET GO OF YOUR PRIDE

I have a saying, "Pride is fatal."

I don't say this lightly. Pride is a 'humiliation' magnet. It draws in circumstances that will humble and ground you. Take it from a master of humiliation.

As I started to reflect on my past and look at all the moments that seemed to be horrible, terrible, or awful, I found there was a common thread amongst every single circumstance. This proved to be profound in many ways.

Each time I was humiliated, embarrassed or victimised was a moment right after I was behaving in a proud, egotistic or over-confident manner.

I had an inflated sense of self and was filling myself up with hot air like a balloon. I was filling myself with so much air that I was ready to take to the skies and look down at everyone else – metaphorically. Like a self-righteous royal, peering down at all of the peasants beneath me. So what happened next?

My proud behaviour attracted the attention of others who saw me in a different light. So much so, they felt naturally compelled to humble me and poke a big hole in my balloon to make sure I didn't get 'carried away' by my inflated ego.

The phrase 'don't get carried away' has more meaning than you may realise. The more you focus on building yourself up or inflating your ego with 'hot air', the more you'll become a humiliation magnet and attract situations that are meant to ground you, sometimes literally.

Tripping over and falling down can be another example of being grounded. By falling over, you're hitting the ground. You'll most likely find that right before you tripped and fell over, you were thinking or saying big things about yourself, inflating your ego in some way. But as Sir Isaac Newton proved with his laws of gravity, what goes up must come down.

For every person that thinks the world of you, there is someone who believes you're a nuisance. For each person who believes you're a saviour, there is someone who believes you're a burden. For every fan, there's a critic. Sometimes it takes more than one person to maintain the balance of challenge and support. Even for this very book, there are those of you who feel as though I have helped in a valuable way. There are also others who are frustrated and annoyed by the same insights that I've written. To them, it's something they don't want to confront and that's okay.

Another example is injuries. Think of a time you experienced an injury and the moments before. You were probably being arrogant and over-confident about something. This doesn't mean you should stop trying. It simply means staying humble to the truth that you have an equal degree of strength and weakness that keeps you balanced. If you feel yourself being inflated by others, look around for who is counter-balancing them. Maintain an awareness of the balance around and inside of you, and soon you'll begin to master your life.

If you're at the whim of other's praise and condemnation, you're not a master of your life. You're susceptible to the acceptance and rejection of others. They are an unwitting master of you. That has single-handedly been one of the most destructive things in my own life. Masters do what they can to self-govern. Their compass is managed from within and they use external references as guide posts, signs and warnings.

Whenever you take action or make a decision based on whether people will accept or reject you, you're indirectly dismissing and devaluing yourself. You're saying to yourself, their opinion of you is more important than your own opinion of yourself. The truth is, you make yourself vulnerable when you're attached to your sense of pride. It's brilliantly paradoxical.

You will be criticised and praised no matter what you do, it's unavoidable. The key to mastering this game is to see both sides as they play out and deliberately choose what you want to be praised and criticised for.

Now, if you're feeling proud of what you've achieved and see yourself as a hero in some sense, then you're most likely going to hit a snag, trip over – figuratively or physically – and get humbled. Use this to your advantage. You're being taught a lesson on your behaviour and being given the opportunity to master the balance and moderation of your pride and shame.

The most effective way I've been able to manage this truth in my own life is by realising something that my wife woke me up to. I would spend a weekend at a workshop with my mentor, helping people break through their self-imposed beliefs and perceptions, much like I am in these pages. They'd let go of their fears, shame and guilt and start appreciating themselves for who they truly were and transform their perceptions of the experiences they'd had.

In my early days of these workshops, I would come home feeling a sense of pride for what I had done for these people, not aware that I was about to walk right into an argument with my wife. She'd bring stuff up that I had forgotten about, ignored or just showed no sense of care for. At first, I would say, "Why are you bursting my bubble? Why are you trying to ruin this for me?" But then as I woke up to what was really happening, I had nothing but deep-seated appreciation for her.

She wasn't aware of it at the time but she was grounding me. She was keeping me humble, making sure I didn't get 'carried away'. It truly was a gift from her. So I decided to do it for myself. Whenever I was coming home from something that I was feeling particularly proud about, I would take a few minutes to run through my head to find where I had dropped the ball during that day.

"Did I forget to reply to a message? Did I return the calls I said I would? Did I get back to the people I promised? Did I say thank you to the people who helped me in some way? Did I avoid paying a bill or invoice because I didn't think it was important enough? Did I ignore someone that wanted something from me?" I'd ask all these questions to look for behaviour that wasn't something I could be proud of. It was a way to self-regulate my pride and shame, and to humble myself. If we don't regulate our own pride and shame, people and circumstances will do it for us. It helps maintain the conservation of balance.

So by humbling my pride on my way home from these workshops, I would free my wife from having to unconsciously ground and humble me. Instead, we'd be grateful to see each other and talk about the day we'd just had. The playing field was level. There was no high ground, which made our time together deeper and more rewarding.

It looked like I was doing it for myself but I was actually setting her free from having to be the person who grounds and humbles me whenever I got proud. She noticed the change and started to thank me for it. She didn't like having to play that role so consistently for me, so by self-governing my pride with an equal amount of humility, I was alleviating her from the burden of having to play that role in my life.

If someone is grounding you, you probably need it, and if you're too proud to admit it then you most definitely need it. The world around you is attempting to keep you centred because who you really are is found at the centre of your emotions, not at the extreme ends of the emotional pendulum.

Become grateful for the people keeping you humble. They're stopping you from getting carried away by the strong winds of your ego as the hot air balloon rises to extreme heights. Think of them as the all-important sand bags hanging off the side of the hot air balloon basket. Without them, you won't be able to return to solid ground when you need to. But too many of these humble sand bags and you won't ever take off to new places.

"Anger is an acid that can do more harm to the vessel in which it is stored than to anything on which it is poured."

MARK TWAIN

GIVE USE TO YOUR ANGER AND FRUSTRATION

Anger and resentment are interesting emotions. If allowed, they can take over the mind and start driving the decisions and actions we make or don't make. This can be destructive in certain situations, professional or otherwise.

Like all things in the world, if anger and resentment weren't needed then they would have no reason to exist. So if that's the case, what purpose do they serve? The answer: discontent. Anger and resentment can move you out of apathy and forward with momentum.

Typically you'll start with a restlessness. As if you have something bothering you under your skin. Something trying to escape you. That's because there's a part of you itching to get out, to find its way out into the world. It wants out and you're subconsciously suppressing it. The internal dictator is saying, "No! You cannot say that! That's not what we do. We're safe, secure, stable and won't be rocking any boats with that nonsense." However, the more you suppress something, the more the pressure builds and the more turbulent your mind becomes.

That's in part what your anger and resentment are. You've been suppressing your thoughts and emotions. Making sure they simmer but with the lid on, so there's no bubbling and spitting from the pot. At some point, the lid will blow off and you'll have a bigger mess to clean up.

That's when anger steps in. It gets you out of your suppressive state and into your expressive state. The problem is, it's the opposite extreme and is typically not managed well. Meaning, the anger takes over and starts to run the show, which is just as counterproductive as letting the suppressive part of you shut down your expression.

Following me so far?

Allow me to give you a story to help my point. For years I sat at an office desk doing the 'safe' thing. Dealing with my 'responsibilities' and earning my income, keeping my day job and paying my expenses. All while there was a huge part of me itching to share what I knew with people. All of the things I've written in this book and much, much more were eagerly waiting to be shared.

But I had that inner voice saying, "Stay safe, you can't afford to make any more mistakes or take any more risks with your professional life." While I was suppressing what I wanted to express, I felt this simmering discontent itching to unshackle and let my heartstrings loose for people to experience. How though? I couldn't see the path to get me there other than pouring myself into these pages.

As I did that, I gave myself space to breathe and ease my discontent. Then it would come back as I moved further down the path of writing this book. The discontent started to brew and build heat. It was causing more of a discomfort and making me restless. By trying to stop myself from experiencing that restlessness, I would feel it get worse.

It was my suppression, but in another form. So I decided to let the restlessness brew into a frustration, the frustration build into anger and the anger distil into complete discontent. I stopped trying to control the feeling and decided to lean into it to see what it was attempting to teach me.

Whether it's towards another person, yourself or your work situation, when discontent strikes, it's because you're not permitting what you want for yourself.

Let the discontent settle in. Give it a place in your life and then use it to get where you want. Is the discontent surfacing something you need to address in your relationship? Something at work? The people you're spending your precious time with? The project you started but never finished or the project you keep putting off? Or maybe the destination you haven't allowed yourself to visit and explore? They're all different forms of complacency.

Complacency is a dangerous place to live. It's a place many people choose to live in. We weren't meant to be complacent, we weren't meant to rest on our laurels. That's not how progress works. It's time to move forward. Complacency is like a staircase landing. It's a great place to rest, not set up residence. No one wants to live their life on a staircase landing. Climb to the top so you know what's up there and then you can choose where you want to be. Just make sure you explore the full staircase.

Your discontent is helping you. Instead of shutting it down, use it to get where you're ready to move on to. Use your discontent to set yourself free from delusional beliefs keeping you living a small life. They'll stop serving you sooner than you realise.

Personal empowerment and freedom take place inside of the individual who realises they have no justified reason to subordinate their soul to the ideas and opinions of others. Like a ship subordinating itself to an anchor. The anchor is there to serve, not become an obstacle.

"When you are content to be simply yourself and don't compare or compete, everybody will respect you."

LAO TZU

STOP COMPARING YOURSELF TO OTHERS

Self-comparison creates an unruly mess in the minds of many. Have you ever looked at someone's accomplishments or possessions and wished you had what they have?

This can be characteristics or material things. Either way, your envy or admiration for what they have in their lives will make you blind to your own wealth and trigger an immediate depreciation for what you *do* have. You'll almost completely write off what you have worked your whole life for.

This self-comparison runs rampant in the personal development world and I've witnessed it amongst a lot of my peers and even some mentors. They'll uncover some revelation and deep insight into their behaviour, clear out any emotional baggage around the pattern and free themselves of any of the mindset blocks that hold them back. Then they move on, parading all of their achievements and successes in their lives, heralding their accomplishments like badges of honour. What's wrong with doing this? Nothing, except that these badges can become burdens over time.

To me, and other insightful people, what's taking place is obvious. Once they overcome their obstacles, they find themselves having no excuse to go and do what they'd love to, so then they compare their lives with the life of someone they look up to and admire. Once engaged in this self-comparison, they find themselves feeling small about how 'little' they've achieved in comparison and compensate for this feeling by parading their accomplishments and over-exaggerating what they've done in their lives.

Keeping up?

They're caught in a vicious cycle which they aren't aware of. That is, they're overcompensating for how their lives look in comparison to the life of the person they look up to. My question is: Is that being authentic?

They're not owning what they see in their idol, mentor, teacher or leader. They're suppressing their own inner genius in relation to this person. That is what comparison is.

Here's what the wise Ralph Waldo Emerson says in his essay on Self-Reliance published in 1841...

"There is a time in every man's education when he arrives at the conviction that envy is ignorance; that imitation is suicide; that he must take himself for better for worse as his portion; that though the wide universe is full of good, no kernel of nourishing corn can come to him but through his toil bestowed on that plot of ground which is given to him to till."

What does this mean?

It means the rewards and wealth you reap from your life come from making the most of what's given to you in your character, your willingness and your self-belief. It has nothing to do with what everyone else is doing. What Emerson is also saying is that, in order for you to be able to go and get whatever you want in your life, you first have to accept what you have. Appreciate what you have, who you are, both the good and the bad, before you go seeking to change anything. It'll make a world of difference to the life you create.

Your envy, jealousy and admiration reflect your ignorance to the fact that those people are doing one of two things:

1. They're overcompensating and self-promoting to make themselves feel better about their unfulfilled life and the lack of inspiration that they perceive in their life.

2. They're truly living a life congruent with themselves irrespective of what others think of them. They're ignorant to the praise and criticism they receive.

In my view, modern technology has given the everyday person the ability to promote a life that isn't whole and complete, which fuels this self-destructive behaviour. Did the technology cause this behaviour? No. It just amplified the behaviour of society which had existed long before. Hence the long-held idiom 'keeping up with the Joneses'. Self-comparison has lasted throughout societies of all kinds.

The reason I say it's self-destructive is because by placing other people on a pedestal you're subconsciously desiring to destroy what you have. You want to shut it down, throw it away or simply pretend you don't have what you have due to inner shame. This will ensure you never get what they have — a self-fulfilling prophecy. Why would you receive more when you're not grateful for what you already have?

These people you compare yourself to are your reflection. They're showing you a part of yourself that you've been disowning. That changes today.

“No star wears a veil.”

MARCUS AURELIUS

DISCOVER YOUR INNER GENIUS

We all like irony. It makes us chuckle to ourselves about how things seem contradictory while making complete sense at the same time. When I was a young boy, people didn't know how to pronounce my surname. Whether it was teachers, doctors, friends or other kids at school, they all struggled for some reason. Because they didn't know how to pronounce my surname, I would usually get the name Giorgio Genius.

I continue to get that even as an adult. My computer, to this day, tries to autocorrect the spelling of my surname to Genius. Up until the rough age of twenty-two, I would think it was a bad name. I used to think that being a genius was something to be made fun of. Like I was too smart for my own good and that made me a geek in some way.

When I was twenty-two I realised that being a genius was a gift. It was something that was instilled in me. From where? I won't say. That's not important. What's important here is that I believed that maybe this surname was in some way predestined for me. In some way, it was to become a duty, a responsibility for me to live with. Not because I believe that I'm particularly smarter than anyone else but because I have the ability to show anyone that they're a genius, no matter how much they believe otherwise. What was once something I disowned has now become somewhat of a superpower.

I should note that my Dad had changed his surname in the 1970s as a way to make it easier for the Anglo-Australians to pronounce his Greek surname. His efforts didn't work. It made things significantly more complicated. But what he did is start a new family name that doesn't exist and in his own way, whether realising it or not, he helped me earn a cool nickname that aligns with the way I spend my life.

While I was gifted the nickname of being a genius, I wasn't sure that it was true. I wasn't sure that I could possess the qualities of being a genius or that I had genius within me. As I developed a sense of self-awareness, I was able to reflect on different experiences in my life and see that there was a common thread to the way I applied myself to life. No matter what it was, I had a unique way of thinking and approaching life's problems.

At those times I thought everyone else would think, act and see the way I did. I learned later on that it wasn't true. So because of this, I inspected my past and found common threads running throughout my life. No matter what I was doing at the time I had a similar approach to everything I did. Through realising this, I learned that it is exactly that — my approach to life, my approach to whatever I do — that is my genius. It's not what I do but how I do it. That's what makes me a genius. This led me to think that perhaps because everyone thinks differently to one another that everyone must be endowed with genius. Wouldn't they? Aren't you?

The answer is yes, you are. You have a genius within you. You possess the qualities of a genius. You may be reading this thinking I'm crazy or just trying to motivate you into some delusion, but that's not the case. Before I go into the details of how to reveal your inner genius and your gift, I want you to consider something. Nature has a way of taking care of everything. The order that guides the processes of nature has a way of making sure there's a purpose and meaning to all things, including you.

If you didn't have something both unique and purposeful to contribute, why would you be here? We all have something and it's no mistake. I'm calling it a gift. Others call it a duty or responsibility. Whatever name you give it, you have it. That gift that you possess is what underlies your genius. It's your 'thing', your calling.

Now it's time to go digging. Grab your mental shovel so we can get started. Be warned – this may make you see yourself differently. By differently I mean you may actually be inspired by who you are.

First up, let's look at all the different ways people have complimented your efforts on something. Run through your life like you're watching a movie and look at the different times people have complimented the way you've done something or your perception about something. They may look like moments when you've thought to yourself that it was no big deal. Moments when you assumed that others do the same thing you do, but it was mentioned to you in a way that made you think it was unique. Write them down. It may only be 3-5 things that you can think of. That's fine, it's a start.

Next up, think of the things that you've done in your life that were easy but fun for you. It could've been tasks you had to do as part of your various jobs at different companies. Go through all your jobs. There was something in each of them that you liked. Something that was easy for you to get through. Even if it was a job you resented, there was something in the role that fulfilled you in some big or small way. Again, there may only be 3-5 things. Some of them may overlap or may be the same thing. That's fine. We're looking for common threads that run throughout what you've done in your life up until this moment.

Another thing you can do is think of the things you did as a child. Go through the games you loved playing, the places you loved visiting and the activities you loved doing. They will have common threads running through them too. In fact, it's highly likely that they're similar, if not identical, to the things that you loved about your different jobs. That's not a mistake.

The reality is that you have been experiencing and expressing your genius since childhood. It's not something that your school or your parents taught you. It's innate. It exists in everyone. Your genius is your gift. You've spent your life expressing it, but what's been tricking you into thinking you don't possess genius is self-comparison, fear, shame, guilt and the belief that only a few people in this world are geniuses. They're all illusions. These will most certainly keep you from recognising and owning your inner genius, but they haven't stopped you from expressing it. That has happened no matter what you've been through in your life. What we're doing here, right now, in these words and these pages is revealing that gift you've been carrying with you through your entire life.

I'm here to show you that there's more inside of you than you realise. It's not a matter of if you have genius, it's a matter of if you can see it.

Like your breathing, you've probably been unconscious about what your genius is. It's been happening in the background without your conscious awareness of it. You haven't had to think about it and you've just kind of plodded your way through each moment of your life. When you become consciously aware of your inner genius and your gift, you wake up to a sense of power and freedom. You wake up to who you are. You see yourself for who you are and the magnificence you possess. I know this sounds like I'm inflating you, trying to motivate you, but this is the truth. The only way for you to truly believe it is to do the work. Reveal to yourself who you truly are. When you become aware of the genius you possess it will seem obvious. Ironically, it's like a huge revelation that isn't really a revelation at all.

Another word for genius is brilliance. In optics, brilliance means to shine. Your inner genius is like an inner light for you. It is the light that has been guiding you through your life, and will continue to guide you throughout the rest of your life. By allowing yourself to express your inner genius, you start to light yourself up. By lighting yourself up, you naturally light up those around you. The ripple effect of living this way is hard to measure, but one thing you can be sure of is that your brilliance will give others permission to express their inner brilliance, their inner genius and their gift. No more hiding from who you are. You're here to shine, to express that light that's inside of you. You're meant to express your genius in your very own unique way. The more you do so, the more your life will feel as though it makes sense to you. Stars don't pretend to be planets and planets don't pretend to be stars. Own your inner genius, no one else will do it for you. Once you do, challenges will become opportunities of expression.

So now I ask you: How will you choose to express yourself, genius?

"Remember that wherever your heart is, there you will find your treasure."

PAULO COELHO

DEVELOP SELF-BELIEF

Let's get something out of the way. When I refer to self-belief I don't mean confidence. Confidence is the by-product, the sum or the result of having self-belief and self-worth. Why is this distinction important? Because you've come here looking for confidence. I'm telling you that you don't need confidence. Everyone has confidence. But if the thing that's responsible for confidence – self-belief – isn't present, then confidence will have no ground to stand on, falling into a pit that seems to have no bottom.

The word belief stems from the Dutch word *lief* which translates to loveable. Interesting? I hope so.

Self-belief has nothing to do with how confident you are, how charismatic or social you are. It has nothing to do with Type-A personalities and it's certainly got nothing to do with your level of intellect. It has everything to do with your ability to love yourself. I don't mean the ability to inflate yourself, but to love yourself. To see yourself as the purposeful individual you are. To see yourself as the complete you, warts and all, and still be able to love what you see. It's hard to do, right? Well, our society has an issue with this kind of thinking, which has made it hard for you to learn the importance of self-belief. Not to worry. It's more a reflection of their own journey than yours.

Self-belief comes from within. Hence the word *self*. You will have a variety of people throughout your life who believe in you. At times they'll show a belief that seems greater than your own. What you'll notice is that no matter how much others believe in you, they can't keep it up forever; otherwise, your ability to live your life becomes dependent on others' belief in you. It's not sustainable. Building your own foundation for self-belief makes it easier for you to stand comfortably on solid ground. It creates the platform from which you live your life.

The hardest part about building that foundation is laying the groundwork. Doing so requires that you dig and that you dig deep. You'll have to dig down into the mud and create long trenches. If we're going to build a foundation of self-belief, we want to make sure it's solid and that it won't crumble at the slightest challenge or tremor.

You struggle to believe in yourself because no matter what you say about how great you are, when you look at yourself you see all your faults. You see all that's wrong and all of the failures you had while you so easily forget the triumphs. (For more on overcoming your failures go to page 309.) Put another way, you see yourself and you struggle to believe that you are enough.

You as you are – the good, the bad, the pretty, the ugly, the weak, the strong, the boring, the fascinating, the sweet, the bitter, the cruel, the kind, the frustrating and the amusing –all these parts of who you are make you enough. Read that again.

When you judge yourself you only see a portion of who you are. You take it out of context and distort the truth. It's like the scattered pieces of a jigsaw puzzle. It looks overwhelming. It takes up a lot of space. It looks chaotic and doesn't appear to make up a complete picture. By viewing yourself as scattered pieces, you sell yourself a story that you're willing to buy and you keep coming back for more. What if I said that by looking further into the story you've been telling yourself, you'll find something different?

What if you find something that is completely different to the narrative you've been telling yourself? What if the truth is that you, the complete you, the collection of all of your parts, the coalescence of all your traits, is what makes you enough?

What if at the times in your childhood when you developed the belief that you aren't enough, you reassessed your experiences and found that you were actually learning that you are enough?

Would that help you harness self-belief? Would that make for solid foundations? Would that make it more natural for you to love yourself for all that you are? Your answer better be yes, otherwise I wrote this for nothing.

Those times in your past when you developed the belief that you aren't enough are distortions of the truth. They're stories you bought into, and you have become so used to them that no amount of force will bring change. After a few days of trying to change your thinking, you bounce back like a rubber band.

So here's what I want you to do in order to create solid foundations. Look back at different times that you felt in some way you weren't enough. At those moments, you only believed you weren't enough and ignored the other side of the truth. You weren't seeing the whole picture. So ask yourself now how you *were* enough in those moments. What was going on? Was someone saying something to you? Were they doing something? Were you doing or saying something yourself? Whatever it was that was taking place, look for the clue in that moment that was suggesting the opposite. Where's the clue that was left behind that suggests you are enough?

For example – when I was a young boy, I used to get night terrors and didn't like sleeping alone in my bedroom. I would wake up at some stage during the night and freak out. The loneliness compounded the feeling and triggered panic. After a while, I didn't like the idea of sleeping alone so I would ask my mother each night if I could sleep in bed with her and Dad. As a child it was a no-brainer, for my parents it was a different story. They, like most parents, preferred to sleep without getting kicked and woken up. When Mum told me that it wasn't okay to sleep in their bed, I took it as "I'm not good enough." Almost like a rejection. This left an impression on me and made the panic worsen each night. Her intentions were to help me overcome my fears and become more self-reliant. I didn't understand that at the time. When I became wise enough I did the exercise above and realised that I wasn't being rejected. Mum wasn't rejecting me or telling me I wasn't good enough to sleep in their bed. What she was actually telling me was that I was more than capable of sleeping alone, handling the night as it unfolded, and that I was going to be okay because I was enough. (Worst case scenario was that I go and wake her up if I had a panic attack.) I wasn't giving myself a chance because I was too scared to explore what she was trying to show me.

The truth is, the way you interpret the situation is what shapes your beliefs. (Read the chapters on beliefs (page 23) and perceptions (page 33).) By giving yourself the chance to change what you see at these 'defining' moments, you give yourself the opportunity to completely alter your beliefs. Especially beliefs that involve self.

In each moment life is guiding you to value and love yourself. To see yourself for the brilliance that you are. Giving yourself an opportunity to change the way you see yourself in the past can be the single most life-altering experience you can ever have. You'll end up loving more of who you are, which will give you the solid foundation you've been looking for. Besides, with the strength of self-belief (self-love), imagine what you can build when the foundation is strong enough to hold you up. You are enough. Now it's time to build.

3

YOUR BODY

“Our own physical body possesses a wisdom which we who inhabit the body lack. We give it orders which make no sense.”

HENRY MILLER

LISTEN TO WHAT YOUR BODY IS SAYING

It doesn't always seem true but your body is communicating with you constantly. It's been written about for centuries, long before microscopes were able to peer into the lives of the cells that make up our bodies. I'll save the anatomy, physiology and biology lesson for the textbooks, but I will touch on the topic of the language your intuition uses.

I'll start with a quick note on intuition for those of you who have attached a stigma to the word. It means *to have a perception of truth without the use of reason.* Meaning, the ability to perceive with a knowledge and intellect that is beyond logical thoughts.

Your body has pre-existent and built-in wisdom or, what some call, an innate intelligence. Meaning, it's really clever. Clever beyond your knowing and the current knowledge of science. Proof of that last point can be made by looking at the scientific discoveries made regularly about some of the functions that take place within the body. We're forever discovering something new, which means we're discovering just how much we don't know.

Cultures throughout history all had a different name for this innate intelligence, but all of them acknowledged its existence in some way. Let's look at the basics for a moment. If all you did was eat well, fend off immediate danger and manage to get by without major, life-threatening disease, you'll most likely last several decades of life. I'm sure you know people who have lived this way. Rarely visiting a doctor, and not really having much to report when it comes to illness and problems. This being true, consider all of the constant changes, functions and battles that take place within that person's body. The endocrine (hormone) system is regulating energy, appetite, satiety, rest and libido. The digestive system is killing pathogenic bacteria in your food and adding the right mixture of chemicals to extract and absorb essential nutrients, all whilst keeping your previous meals moving, using the fluids and water necessary to clean your blood, filter toxins and eliminate harmful waste. Your spine houses the vital passageway for your brain and body to communicate with each other, and it's constantly rebuilding itself to make sure the tiny electrical charges carrying important messages reach your organs, muscles and immune system while allowing these systems to simultaneously report crucial messages back to the brain. This is happening while your muscles obligingly take orders to contract and relax as you make your way to the bathroom and relieve your over-stretched caffeine-loaded bladder, because it knew to speak up at the right time to ensure infection didn't take place causing overloaded stress to your kidneys and immune system.

These are only a tiny fraction of the functions which happen multiple times a day, every single day, for you to maintain existence, and you haven't had to pick up the instruction manual once to figure out how to make it all work. It just works. It harmoniously functions with the grace of a ballet dancer carrying decades of experience on stage. It's clever and it hasn't taken a single day off.

My personal belief is that you would be wise to take a moment each day to thank your body for carrying you through that day and doing whatever is necessary to keep you alive without you having to micromanage every tiny little function. Imagine a company that makes a product that you can keep for the rest of your life and doesn't send out an instruction manual because it's completely self-regulating. That's your body and the company is infinite intelligence, the universe, GOD, and all other variations of the same thing.

So, what would this marvellous organism need to tell us or communicate to us if it's so masterful at self-regulation? Well, that's the beauty of it. Your intuition uses your body to communicate the messages you've been ignoring.

Keep in mind, there are hundreds of books which talk of symptom-specific causes and allopathic remedies for your conditions. I'm simply referring to the subtle, unnoticed messages that you're getting long before they become serious, more immediate and attention-worthy problems.

Let's say you've just had a confrontation with someone and it's left you with 'knots' in your stomach. It feels like someone has literally twisted your stomach into a knot, it's become so tight and small. That's your intuition telling you that you're not okay with what just happened and that it's wise for you to do something about it.

Or let's say you're waking up fatigued day after day and you've noticed it only started a couple of weeks ago. Each day your energy plummets and you're craving all kinds of comfort food to make you feel better about your lethargy.

Or maybe you seemingly developed a tense shoulder and neck that's been keeping you awake at night because you can't get comfortable and pain-free enough to close your eyes.

These, amongst most other issues, are your intuition suggesting there's something for you to learn and it would be wise to listen to its messages.

Why does your intuition use your body to give you messages? Because you're ignoring the subtle ones. Your intuition is whispering to you in each moment. It has something to tell you to help guide you through your life, but if you're not listening you won't hear it. Think of a party – there's a house full of people talking, laughing, making loud noises and there's music filling in whatever silence is left. Through all of that, there's someone at this party who has some very profound and interesting things to tell you. However, they only speak in whispers because what they have to say is for you and no one else to hear. There are times when the room gets louder with noise but your whispering friend doesn't change their volume, yet their whispers continue. The whisperer is your intuition. It won't raise its voice directly, it'll just change the way it talks.

If your head is filled with mindless and endless dialogue, like the party, you'll never hear the whispers of your intuition. Quietening your mind will make it easiest to hear your intuition. Now, if you haven't developed your way of quietening your mind or you're just ignoring your intuition, then it'll turn to your body for its next form of communication. It's still subtle but it's more likely to get your attention. The problem is, in most cases, people typically go to a doctor and use painkillers to shut it up as opposed to working out what exactly their intuition is attempting to tell them. To me, doing this is like covering up the 'check engine' light on the car when the warning comes up. This covering of the engine light implies that people know more about the body than the body itself. It implies that the body is a stupid mechanism and that we know better. What gets forgotten is that the body has taught humanity and will continue to, not the other way around.

Usually, just before the symptoms emerged, something would have likely happened that you didn't respond to with a balanced perspective. This is also known as a trigger. Life's problems are mostly about how you're responding to them. If your response isn't one of 'thanks' or gratitude, then it's usually some form of stress. If you're perceiving it as stressful then you're missing half the picture – the other side of the polarity – and your intuition is doing what it can to get you back to the centre. Living in *distress* means the two halves of the poles have been split in your mind. *Di* – meaning cut – *stress*.

Here's a prime example – there was a point in my life when I was waking up exhausted. It was as if I hadn't slept and had spent the night awake reading or watching TV. The problem to most people would seem that I'm not getting enough sleep or that I was overworking. But the truth was, that nothing had really changed except for one verbal exchange which had an effect on me. What followed was lots of adrenaline, and it threw off my body's chemical balance. This had an impact on my sleeping and because I wasn't able to rest and recover while I was asleep, I was waking up exhausted, in fight/flight mode when it was meant to be in rest and repair mode. Doing this for several days on end was costing me my physical wellbeing. I eventually got to a point where I spent most of my Sunday on the lounge resting because I couldn't keep myself up.

I ended up sacrificing my time with my wife, I didn't have the energy to go for my walks and I couldn't lather up the social energy to go to a picnic I was invited to. I did choose to listen to my body, though. I rested because it was telling me to rest. Once I had rested I went looking for the cause of my fatigue. It was a conversation I had had with an advisor who pushed me to a level I was totally uncomfortable with. The problem wasn't what was being suggested to me, it was how I saw it. My perspective was one-sided and my intuition was telling me that my perspective needed a shift so I could see the whole situation for what it was, which would make it easier for me to make a clear decision and act on it. All I saw was a problem and my intuition was telling me that there's a solution as long as I change my perspective. Until that moment it was all party noise and drowned-out whispers.

To put it simply, typically, there's a trigger: emotional, chemical or physical. If it's emotional, which is more often than you think, it's likely to be something that requires a perspective shift. Shift your perspective, see both sides of the situation, gain an overview and your intuition won't have to use your body to tell you what you've been ignoring.

P.S. Let me be clear about my position on physical wellbeing so there's no room for assumptions. The allopathic healthcare model — treating symptoms instead of the cause of the symptoms — has a place in this world. It has saved lives and has enabled people to live a life that wouldn't have been possible otherwise. Using the allopathic method doesn't serve well in the support of the body's natural abilities to adapt and evolve. It's not effective in preventative wellbeing. This chapter is here to help the body and the mind work together, to work in conjunction with other forms of healing. This isn't just a disclaimer, it's my personal belief based on personal experience.

Use the best of both worlds to balance out your physical, chemical and psychological stress so you're not depending on either of the methods completely. Also, educate yourself on the body. Informing yourself about the body and the mind can be two of the most empowering experiences you can have. It's time to start trusting that there's wisdom inside your body that we as a species haven't tapped into yet.

Your intuition is using whatever means necessary to get through to you. At some point you'll be forced to listen. Don't wait for the hospital bed to finally hear it. You don't have to.

"We should eat to live, not live to eat."

MOLIÈRE

EAT TO LIVE

We've come to an interesting point in societal development. A time when entertainers influence everyday people and chefs have become idolised celebrities. Meals have become a form of entertainment and staged experience, while people are regularly consuming a variety of foods through their mouths and their eyes.

Diet has had its meaning redeveloped from 'a way of life' into 'restriction from variety'. New scientific discoveries have swarms of people running from one food type to another, stressing their bodies from one extreme state to the next. Somewhere along the way, people went from eating to live, to living to eat. How it happened is almost irrelevant to the point that I'm making here.

What I'm more interested in addressing is why people eat what they do and why they avoid eating what they don't.

Years ago, I was wrestling with my experiences in life and it was affecting my body. I had all kinds of digestive issues, headaches, fatigue and other symptoms that were affecting my day-to-day life. I was told to cut out a variety of foods, change what I was eating and how often I ate. As I started to explore nutrition and some of the upcoming research that was popular at the time, I bought into the demonisation of different food types and the way they were being produced. This was restrictive yet educational.

What I didn't realise at the time was that I was developing a perception of different foods. I was beginning to judge certain foods and so whenever I was exposed to the food, my body would have a reaction to it. If I ate it, I would bloat, get gas, have digestive cramps and it would affect my bathroom visits. This reinforced my judgment of the food and led to further avoidance. Basically, it led to further dietary restriction which meant I was limiting my nutritional variety and creating nutrient deficiencies in my body. To make up the difference, I was using a concoction of dietary supplements. The supplements helped fill in the gaps but didn't resolve the underlying issue — the avoidance of certain foods. The supplements helped but they had big gaps to fill. Supplements are meant to do exactly that, supplement a broad-spectrum nutritional plate.

It was my study of human behaviour and psychology that woke me up to the impact that our thoughts about food have on how our body reacts to the food we eat. Here's what I've found with my clients and my own life experiences.

You typically have some kind of psychological association with the foods you have a physical reaction to.

I often see people who have reactions to different foods and they just assume that they have some intolerance or allergy to it. More often than not, there's a psychological association that's determining their body's reaction to the food.

Now, let's dig into this. Your tonsils are your first line of defence when you consume food. They're loaded with immunity inspectors that mark harmful foods with red flags to let the immune system know that there's an intruder coming down the pipe. As the food makes its way through your digestive system, it will be confronted by the immune system's disarming tactics. The immune system will do whatever's necessary to ensure the body stays alive and is capable of functioning. Sometimes this means rejecting the food through the vomiting reflex; other times it means increasing mucus in the intestinal tract to move the food through as quickly as possible and out of the body, without taking the time to absorb the water content and nutrients – also known as diarrhoea.

On the other hand, when food is not recognised as a threat, it is welcomed, nurtured and assimilated so the body can use every part of the food that it can in order to survive and thrive.

As an over-generalisation, your body is governed by your nervous system, which is governed by your brain, which is managed by consciousness. Nervous system —> brain —> mind.

A prime example of this is the adrenaline response. If you perceive someone or something as a threat, it stimulates the amygdala in the brain that engages the fight/flight/freeze response and tells the adrenal glands to dump adrenaline into the bloodstream. All of this could be triggered because you saw a big black dog without a leash. This increases your heart rate and your breathing rate to help get blood and oxygen to your muscles to help you run or fight your way to survival.

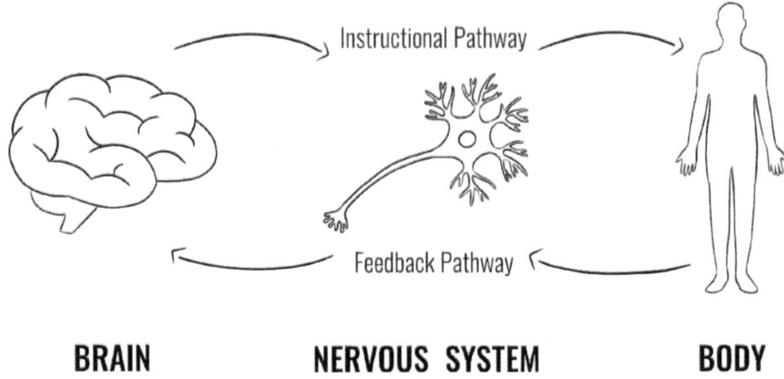

I've found the same to be true with food reactions. Assuming the food is safe to eat (not loaded with dangerous pathogens or toxins), if you perceive food to be a threat, you're going to stimulate an immune reaction in the body to address the food according to the way you see it.

I like to use the example of lactose intolerance because it's common for people to have this kind of food intolerance. I had a client who had a strong reaction to milk and dairy foods. No matter what form the dairy was in, as long as they ate it, they were sure that they would have to have a lengthy visit to the bathroom soon afterwards.

With one particular case, through a few minutes of questioning, I was able to uncover what their perception of dairy was and then when they developed this perception. In this case, Charlie perceived that dairy ravaged his body. He said, "It just goes through my body and totally ravages my insides." I said to him, "With that perception, how do you expect your body to react to that food?"

Then, through the questions I outline below, we worked out that he had associated milk with his grandmother and that he had a particular memory when he was a child when his grandmother had gotten him into trouble and 'raged' at him for it. He saw her as ravaging him through the act of enforcing her discipline.

Food has a powerful ability to remind you of people you have certain associations with, both good and bad. Whether it's the smell, the taste or texture, it can take you back to a memory in the blink of an eye.

If you eat a lot of a particular food like chocolate and find yourself craving it, it's usually because you have an association of chocolate with someone who used to make you feel good, who ate a lot of chocolate themselves or had a reputation for gifting you a piece whenever you visited.

On the other hand, if you have a strong avoidance of certain foods, you associate that food with someone who challenged and stressed you out, so that food reminds you of them. I can hear your mind connecting the dots already.

Before we go into how to change your perception, I want to reiterate something. Like in Charlie's case, if you perceive something is going to ravage, hurt, damage or challenge your body in some way while you're eating it, how do you think your body is going to treat it? Is it going to treat that food as a friend or foe, a threat or ally, nourishment or poison?

If you're perceiving a food that you're eating as a threat, then you're robbing your body's ability to extract the nutrients it has that will help you live.

You might be thinking, "I'm fine just avoiding the foods I don't like, thanks." I'm saying by removing the limitations of what you 'can' and 'can't' eat, you open up your nutrient palate to help you get more nutrients from more sources, so you can get on with living a life that isn't hampered by the demonisation of food. Food is medicine and it has significantly fewer side-effects than modern medicine. By removing your emotional associations with food, you allow food to be your first line of medicine and relegate the modern forms to be the backup plan instead of your immediate go-to resource.

My own exploration into the world of nutrition has been valuable and enlightening (I'm not a registered nutritionist or dietician). It has taught me a wealth of knowledge about the body's functions – physiology – and that nutrients affect every part of our body. Nothing in the body happens in isolation. Including where medication has impact.

Here are the steps to get clear on your food associations and how to change them.

1. List out the foods that you don't like or the ones you can't stop yourself from eating. The food you avoid or crave.

2. Define what it is about that food that you like or don't like exactly. Is it the texture, the flavour, the smell or a specific part of it?

3. Now define who that food reminds you of. It might be a relative or someone you had a memorable interaction with at some point. There's a memory you have that is strongly associated with that food or a dish with that food in it.

4. Define what that person was doing to you in that memory that was affecting you. If it's a negative reaction to food, define what the person was doing to you that was challenging you. If it's a positive reaction or a craving for that food then define what the person was doing that was making you feel supported.

5. Now for the best part. Look at who or what was playing out the opposite role in the same moment. If someone was challenging you, who was supporting you? If someone was comforting you, who was challenging you? The complementary opposite existed in that moment.

Keep in mind here, that it isn't always some*one*, it could be some*thing*. For example, if your challenge is with peas and you felt like your parents would trap you into eating the peas on your plate, then maybe you perceived that the peas were giving you freedom by not being attached to what you choose to do. When feeling challenged, people sometimes personify inanimate objects.

The opposite was playing out at the same moment, it just takes looking for it. By finding the equal and opposite of what was taking place, you're able to balance out your perception and dissolve the association you have with that food.

By dissolving the association with negatively perceived food, you change your body's reaction to it and it stops perceiving it to be a threat. By dissolving the association with a positively perceived food that gives you cravings, you stop your body seeking it in moments of challenge, breaking the emotional dependency.

Whatever the association is that you have with food or drink, you can immediately change your body's association to it and alter how you perceive your food. Food helps you live. By removing the barriers that get in the way of you eating to live, you're giving yourself a chance to experience the true value that food has to offer you in the form of macro and micronutrients. Then vitamin and mineral supplements can fill in some of the smaller gaps to help you function effectively, instead of the other way around.

Food is nourishment, life and vitality. Remove the stigmas associated with food and it becomes the medicine it was always meant to be.

In the short time I spent working through Charlie's perception of dairy and milk, he went from having gut-wrenching adverse reactions to wanting to drink a glass of milk at the end of our conversation. He told me later that he'd had that glass of milk, years after he'd last had it as a child. He reported he has never had a reaction to dairy since the day we worked on it. Now, if he wants a glass of milk, he'll pour one and take in all it has to offer without the physical reactions.

Your perception of food determines how much of it your body can utilise. Time to change your perception of food. It has so much to give you. Let it be the nourishment and fuel you need to fulfil your life, purpose and mission. The question is: What will you eat now?

"The body is the instrument of the soul. If the piano player is sick, does it help to repair his or her piano?"

GARY ZUKAV

FOCUS WITHOUT EXHAUSTING YOURSELF

Have you ever been working on a project with such focus that when you checked the time, you realised that three hours had passed, not twenty minutes like you imagined? Then there are other times when even sixty seconds feels like an hour. Everyone experiences this in life. You might think that the ability to focus is about attention span, and to some degree it is. It's also equally about time management.

Here's why some tasks that you think will take you two hours to complete can only take twenty minutes if you dedicate your attention to it. If you multi-task, that twenty-minute task will definitely turn into a two-hour slog. Think about the last time you were able to focus on what you were doing for more than twenty minutes. The last time you were able to place all your attention on what was at hand without the nagging pull of wanting to check emails, messages, the weather forecast, what sales were on and if money had magically appeared into your bank account. The last time you did that was probably a while ago, right?

It's not because there's something wrong with you or that you're nutritionally deficient. It's that you're not fully connected to and involved in what you're doing. Basically, it's not important to you. You don't place much value on it. Well, at least in comparison to the things that are 'distractions'. Let's face it, modern society makes it difficult to live distraction-free. Unless you've taken control of your notifications, your technology is probably very effective at distracting you. The problem isn't the distraction so much as it is your attention. Or your awareness of your attention.

For example, if I told you that if you focus on the task that you keep distracting yourself from doing, I would give you $1,000,000, there's a good chance you'd focus. We just placed more value on your task than your distractions. We made the reward greater than the pain of focussing. It doesn't have to be money. The reward could be the cost of groceries not being a concern for a year or having someone take care of doing the laundry, having a personal assistant for a year or promising that by the end of the task your anxiety will have dissolved completely.

If you associate more reward than pain with the task, the focus required to complete it will emerge naturally and effortlessly. That's because you see more value in focussing on whatever the task is than on distracting yourself. You actually want to complete it.

Here's a personal example. Sometimes during the writing of this book, I would procrastinate and distract myself from starting another chapter. I would find all kinds of ways to take myself away from doing the task. Even removing all distractions from my office didn't work. All that would make me do is leave my office to find a fitting distraction. So instead, I chose to bring distractions into my office. I left them all around my desk, my bookshelves and even on the floor. I did everything I could to make it easy for distractions to pull me away from writing another chapter. Then, before I'd start another chapter, I would remind myself why I started writing this book in the first place. I reminded myself of the image I would have in my mind of you holding this book and you realising something profound and meaningful about yourself. The meaning and purpose of that one idea in my mind raised the value of writing another chapter so high that everything else melted away. The world melted away. The weather, my stomach, my bladder, my eyes, my posture, the noises and even the music I was playing disappeared and I would power through, typing like I had something meaningful to say. Effortlessly moving my way through my task because I knew that you would read this and apply it to your own life.

This one thought provided the energy, focus and persistence needed to allow the words to flow through me and onto this page. Why? Because it matters a lot to me that you're holding this in your hands. Granted, there are tasks that I struggle with. Tasks that take a longer amount of time than necessary to get through. Things that don't matter as much to me that I find distractions for. But as soon as I realise I'm distracting myself, I look for meaning in what I'm doing. I look for value, purpose and necessity in my task and this makes all else fall away for the time needed to focus.

Those times you feel exhausted from focussing so much is usually because you've had to push yourself to maintain focus. By pushing yourself, you're working against your own natural efforts and exerting a large amount of energy on trying to stay focussed. Or rather, you spend a lot more time trying to not be distracted, which is in itself a distraction and makes the whole task take an exorbitant amount of time. So by the time you get to the end of it, you're exhausted, realising that you got very little done in a very large amount of time. Then you realise how much more you've got to do and that compounds the sense of exhaustion which drives you to look for things to stimulate you. Things like coffee, sugar, soft drinks, liquor, anything online, conversations with people and so on. If the work of staying on track feels difficult, you will find things to 'dis-track' you.

When you look at those times you were focussed without the nagging pull towards distractions, you were probably stimulant free. You were in the zone, working in your flow, ignorant of time, unaware of the world around you, being supported by your own internal energy source, occasionally sipping water because you were breathing through your mouth and it was drying out.

The world didn't exist for you. You were working on what you value, and if it wasn't valuable to you, you managed to connect some degree of value to the task which gave it greater purpose and meaning than any distraction in your life at that time.

The work you do – whether it's related to your family, your social life, your business tasks, taking care of your body, exercising, a creative project, returning to a discipline or maybe a study – has some kind of important value to you. The less value you place on it, the more the distractions seep in like water seeking its own level.

When you genuinely value whatever it is that you're focussing on, you no longer need to focus. You're present with it and when you're fully present, time stops mattering, it stops being a form of measurement. What you're working on becomes what you measure and just working on it gives you a sense of fulfilment.

In the likelihood of you either not knowing how to complete the task or being inefficient at getting it done, you may consider delegating it to someone who knows more about getting it done efficiently. This is, in another way, focussing on your strengths and letting other experts fill in your 'weaknesses'. This might seem reserved for the wealthy, but consider that the wealthy people in society value their time more than they value their money. This is the basis for the simple truth that you can't earn your time back once you've spent it. You can always earn more money.

To put it simply, when you find value in what you're making yourself do, it no longer requires force. If there is no way you can find value in what you're doing, then be prepared to delegate it to someone who does find the task valuable. There's always value to be found in our lives. It's just a matter of knowing where to look and what to look for. When you do, the struggle turns into a game. And the game you're playing develops meaning. Are you ready to play?

"It takes more than just a good looking body. You've got to have the heart and soul to go with it."

EPICTETUS

BECOME COMFORTABLE IN YOUR BODY

Feeling comfortable in your own skin, within your own body, is an often overlooked but important component of your self-image. Self-image means the way you see your complete self, internally and externally. The internal and external self-image influence one another and how comfortable you feel starts on the inside.

You probably don't feel comfortable in your body. I'm confident there are things that you don't like about your body, and not just one or two things, a long laundry list of things you don't like that you would change if you could.

Things like those beauty spots, those scars, those stretch marks, the way your arms look, the shape of your nose, the shape of your chin or cheeks, the asymmetry of your eyes, the wrinkles on your knuckles, how one breast is a little higher than the other, the shape of your smile, the shape of your middle toe, how your glutei (buttocks muscles) aren't perfectly sculpted, the way your chest hair grows and how you've got that little skin tag on your chin.

Some of those were jokes. How did I get so many correct though? Because everyone has issues with their body. Everyone I've worked with has had some degree of body dysmorphia. This is when what you see in the mirror is something that isn't actually there. Body dysmorphia is more common than you think. It has a big impact on how comfortable people feel within their own skin and therefore how they feel around others.

You know that I refer to life's balance in all things. There's a reason for doing so. The value people find in realising life's complementary balance is profound. I've written on end about how we are all filled with a balance of positive and negative characteristics and personality traits. This is not an original concept of mine. Brilliant minds before me have been pointing to it for a long time. The same is true for our body and all of its physical flaws and beauty. We all harbour a balance of physical strengths and weaknesses, beauty and ugliness, attraction and repulsion. I have yet to find someone who doesn't.

I can hear you preparing your argument. Before you get yourself wound up into an emotional pretzel, allow me to elaborate.

People from all walks of life have judgments of their life-vessel (body). Everyone does until they don't. Models, celebrities, world leaders, the attractive beach-goers, the cashier, the nurse, the doctor, the body-builder, the dancer, the performer, the psychologist, the artist and every other roommate on this blue spaceship. What you don't know is that you have as many parts that are attractive as are unattractive.

This is a truth many people wrestle with. How often do you simply write off your beautiful parts because of your unattractive parts? It's where you place your attention and focus. This leads you to develop tunnel vision about your body, and therefore you see nothing other than your physical flaws day in, day out. Eventually, you get to a point where you avoid looking at most parts of yourself when you're in front of the mirror. That's because it's easier to ignore everything than look at the disliked parts and hear your inner judgment and criticism. It's simply an avoidance of pain.

But what if there was no pain to avoid in the first place? What if there was nothing to judge about your body? Imagine that. It has the potential to tear apart a trillion-dollar industry that leverages your pre-existent inner judgment. It's an industry that engages in that conversation you're already having with yourself. You could argue that they know their audience and market better than anyone.

Here's the interesting part. If you saw yourself as being equally attractive and unattractive, where would that leave your inner judgments to live? If you saw your body as a completely balanced form, would you have the option to judge it? Does that allow for judgment to exist? No.

Each time I work through someone's inner judgments about their body, they are left with no room to judge their bodies. They see all the flaws and beauties equally and realise, on a deep level, that their body is exactly as it's meant to be. It's the perfect vessel for their existence. When you're able to realise this for yourself, you have no option but to feel empowered in your own body. You have no other option but to recognise yourself as you. You open up to the body you've been occupying in ways you haven't ever before.

I know how all of this sounds as you read it but I've seen it, time and time again.

Here's how to see the same for yourself. That is, here's how to appreciate the life-vessel you've been in your whole life.

List out all of the parts of your body you judge and dislike. All of them. List every part just like I did above. Be sure to include your judgment. For example, if you don't like your belly, list what about it you specifically dislike. Is it wobbly, fat, wrinkly, big, round, saggy, hairy, etc.?

Now that you've found your judgment of your belly, look for where the opposite exists in or on your body. So if you perceive your belly to be wobbly, what part of your body is firm? If you perceive it to be fat or big, what part of your body is skinny and slim. Your immediate response will be, "Nowhere." I know better though. It just takes closer inspection – which you've avoided.

To continue with the wobbly example, you may have firm toned facial cheeks, firm skin on your arms, firm legs and a firm backside. If you perceive it's fat or big, then look for where you're small and skinny. It might be your eyes, your cheeks, your legs, your feet, your hands, etc. The opposite exists, it's there, it just requires inspection beyond the superficialities that you've been focussed on.

For every judgment you have of a part of your body, you have opposing parts that balance out your judgment. When you realise this, you'll come to appreciate your body – your life-vessel – in a whole new way. How exactly?

You'll come to realise that all of your parts, the good and bad, ugly and beautiful, pleasant and gross all make you perfect. It's the balance of opposites that makes you perfect. It's the two coming together that leads to perfection. A synthesis of duality. You were made from singularity, not duality. You are whole, not dual or split. When you recognise this by doing what I've suggested, you'll recognise that oneness within you and you will feel more capable of being whole.

You will most certainly feel more capable of fully em*bodying* your life vessel. You will become more comfortable within your own skin. You will become less judgmental of what you see and more integrated with who you see in the mirror.

Body dysmorphia in all its extremes and severities is when you look into the mirror and see something other than the truth of who you are and the vessel that you embody. As you go through each of the judgments and balance them out across your body, you will move your perception closer to seeing the perfection that you embody. The centre point between physical pride and shame.

When you see the truth, when you see how perfect your body is as it is, you open a doorway to reveal a whole new version of yourself that you weren't able to see and therefore appreciate. Think of it like keeping yourself stuck in the doorway of a lavish mansion. You've got one foot in the door and one out. How could you possibly come to appreciate this mansion if you're not giving yourself the opportunity to explore everything it has to offer?

This chapter is your chance to explore the mansion that you will spend your whole life in. Step through the doorway, discover what this mansion has to show you. Giving yourself the chance may just prove to you that you've been gifted the perfect home for your soul. It's up to you to decide if you're going to spend your life envious of everyone else's mansion or completely move into yours and take up residence like you were always meant to.

This is your home. Time to get comfortable and appreciative. It has a lot to offer you and it's generous.

"The human body is the best picture of the human soul."

LUDWIG WITTGENSTEIN

UNDERSTAND YOUR SEXUAL SELF

Sexuality is the taboo of the taboo. As difficult as it was to decide if this chapter belonged in the bed of pages with its siblings, I also knew that it had to be written about. You deserve to read the words that follow.

Sexuality in all of its facets and forms is such a repressed topic in western societies. It's understandable, given the apparent authorities throughout history and their views on sexual expression. While I understand why it's been suppressed, I believe in its importance. That's normal.

My sexual expression is vanilla in comparison to the many people I've helped. But as my wife likes to remind me, "Vanilla is the most underrated ice cream flavour." Personally, I'm okay with vanilla because of what you'll read below. Be warned, you're about to get really squirmy and uncomfortable.

Sexuality is a fundamental form of your expression of self-power. People typically start exploring sexuality at a young age, younger than you expect. I'm not talking about the age you were exploring sex with others, I'm talking about the age you started exploring with yourself.

It usually starts with you exploring your body and what's what. You've had your genitals since you were born and you're used to their existence, but up until a certain age you don't really stop, look and explore in-depth. Let's face it, no one is talking objectively about your sexuality to you at a young age. It's usually uncomfortable for the adults to say anything because they're wrestling with their own baggage and judgment around their own sexuality. So the idea of talking to a child about it – especially their own child – is no man's land. It's dangerous territory, so it's easiest for them to not venture at all.

Time and time again, whenever I work with people around the topic of comfortably embodying who they are, there are root causes tracing back to their sexual expression and perhaps, more importantly, the time they first explored their genitals alone. For some, this included masturbation, for others, it was the first time they spent some time inspecting, feeling and learning about their bodies.

Why would your sense of self as a person trace back to this point in your life? Because it was a time when you explored your body and were coming to understand yourself within your body. Like a captain exploring all facets of their ship. Why wouldn't you? You'd want to know what you're working with, wouldn't you?

The typical problem here is the amount of shame and judgment associated with self-exploration and masturbation. Looking up the word in the Oxford dictionary presents the word in an example sentence which says, "We do not like to admit that we masturbate." In some texts, the origin of the word masturbate is believed to stem from the Latin word for defile. Meaning, to damage or spoil. Think about how polarising that is. If you have the belief that self-exploration is a damaging and spoiling act, then what kind of beliefs will you develop as an individual?

Think about it. If you're not allowed to fully understand yourself and your body (your vessel) then doesn't that disempower you? The truth is, your sense of sexuality, your ability to express yourself sexually, is directly tied to your ability to express yourself in other aspects of your life. By removing the shame you feel about exploring and getting comfortable within your body, you're giving yourself permission to be you. If you can't give yourself permission, then no amount of permission or approval from the outside world will be enough. It starts with you, and your sexuality is an important factor in that self-recognised approval.

Most people come away from their first experience of sexual exploration feeling empowered by what they've discovered about themselves. But that sense of empowerment is quickly washed away by shame, guilt and a cloud of confusion. Almost like a line of people came in afterwards all with an opinion and a judgment to share about what just happened. Hopefully, they didn't literally step into the room but instead made their way into the room in your mind. Visitors in your mind can turn into residents if you allow them to get comfortable long enough.

Peel back the layers on all of the shame and guilt you feel about your first time masturbating or just exploring your body and you'll find an empowering experience beneath all of that self-judgment.

There is nothing to be ashamed of when it comes to your sense of sexual exploration and expression. It is a process that is important to your sense of self at a crucial age. Yes, it's meant to be private and yes, it's certainly valuable when done alone at first, because it's usually about you finding out more about you. Then, as your sexual adventures expand, you can learn more from others who can explore with you. When it's done without the shame it can be a fortifying and empowering experience. They can teach you and you can teach them.

Now, to make a comment on the body's reaction to sexual shame. Let's generalise the two major gender hormones – testosterone and oestrogen. Masculinity and femininity. A lot of your body's functions are governed by your nervous system which is governed by your brain. Your brain responds and acts on thoughts, beliefs and perceptions. If you have shame around what it means to be a woman or a man, then your body may very well interfere with the natural expression of the related hormones within your body. When I say interfere, I actually mean follow orders.

For example, if you have shame around being a man, then you may have lower levels of testosterone within your body which can affect a variety of physiological functions, including erections, ejaculation and prostate gland function. The same is true for being a woman. You may be suppressing oestrogen which can impact breast size and egg production along with menstrual cycle severity and consistency. Yes, I can hear you connecting the dots.

Keep in mind, I'm not making any health claims or scientific claims about psychology and the connection to body functions. What I am saying is that I've seen consistency amongst many of my students and clients. Sexuality and its expression are how you identify yourself within your world. Transgender and non-gendered individuals struggle with identity because of the inner conflict that underlies this sense of identity that people derive from their sexuality. It is also something that homosexuals have had to wrestle with for centuries, not to mention heterosexual individuals who have had a once-off homosexual experience.

Whenever there's shame and guilt connected with sexuality, you can be sure there is an inner conflict about whether or not it's okay to be yourself.

To go a step further, sexual expression is also an expression of power. When you feel disempowered in your life, you find that you get power from having sex with another. You may even find that you like to engage in sexually powerful positions and activities to compensate for the overall sense of disempowerment you're experiencing in your life. Think about whether you prefer being on top or not – powerful/submissive.

The same is true for the opposite. If you're feeling particularly empowered in your life, you will be more willing to submit yourself in sexual activities. You may be more willing to let go of control and be 'submissive'. The compensations in the bedroom, or wherever you have sex, are a reflection of how you're feeling about yourself in an aspect of your life that is important to you. Put simply, the empowerment or disempowerment you feel in life is typically reflected in the bedroom.

To change your perception of your sexual expression, go through the chapters on pride (page 127) and guilt (page 119) to help dissolve that emotional weight you carry around your sense of sexuality.

Get comfortable in your sexual expressiveness and your sexual self, then you won't feel the need to chasten yourself for it.

Promiscuity is bred by chastity. Chastity is the result of shame being associated with sexuality. If you have memories from your exploratory youth that you're ashamed of, you will sexually repress yourself as you get older. The more you repress your sexual expression, the stronger your desire will be to express it in inefficient ways that lead to undesired outcomes. This typically looks like sexual promiscuity and desire.

You are ultimately in control of your sense of self and that starts with your ability to accept all parts of who you are, emotionally, physically, psychologically and sexually.

By giving yourself permission to fully express your sexuality, you are telling yourself that it's okay to be the person you are. Your body will then listen to these new instructions and align itself with your newfound beliefs.

Drop the shame, let go of the guilt and allow who you truly are to surface. Your body is yours to own and embody. Do so without the emotional chastity you lock yourself in and your life will become empowered both in and out of the bedroom.

"Many things cause pain, which would cause pleasure if you regarded their advantages."

BALTASAR GRACIÁN Y MORALES

CONTROL THE PANIC

Panic attacks are tender moments. They're an unravelling of the mind and trigger an overwhelm of the nervous system. They are the physical manifestation of impending doom – the sense of imminent death. Enduring a panic attack can be an extremely scary experience, and witnessing a loved one or friend experience a panic attack can be equally so.

While I was in the midst of a panic attack my wife didn't know how to help me. She felt both scared and guilty that she couldn't help me. That's when I realised that the following information was not common knowledge. This is for those of you who don't know how to help someone while they're experiencing a panic attack.

Before I provide any guidance, the following needs to be said. If you are unsure if the person you're with is having a panic attack or dealing with some other condition, contact emergency services. This is not a moment that you want to be playing a guessing game. If you know this is a panic attack because they're prone to them or you have the certainty that it is a panic attack and you want to help them, then consider using any of the following.

Here's what's happening. They're dealing with a high dose of adrenaline circulating through their bloodstream. It happens quickly, so trying to calm this response down can be a little difficult. It triggers an increased heart rate, increased breathing rate, increased oxygen in the blood, blood being drained from their digestive organs and immune system and being redirected towards the limbs for quick response – this is known as the fight or flight response. They may even feel the need to vomit or use the toilet. This is also the body's way of removing unnecessary digestive burdens so it can deal with the perceived threat. Remember, they perceive impending doom. To their nervous system, death is on the horizon. This is why they seem irrational. It goes as far as blood being redirected from the telencephalon – the rational, creative and logical part of the brain – to the amygdala – the part of the brain that deals with vital physiological functions. Panic attacks rarely last more than thirty minutes from beginning to end.

The sense of impending doom is because they perceive that they're being trapped by something or someone and it's going to kill them. It seems irrational but once they're in panic, rationale goes out the window.

What To Do

1. First things first – they feel unsafe and out of control. Find a way to make them feel safe, otherwise it's an uphill battle for both of you. This could mean taking them away from a crowded place, to a park, a seaside spot, into the yard or to a private room like a bathroom, bedroom or meeting room. Feeling watched

during a panic attack heightens the experience, so remove them from having a potential audience if there is one.

2. They'll seem jittery and maybe even physically shaky. Let them pace, bounce their knee up and down, tap their fingers or shake their hands like they're trying to get something out. They have a lot of adrenaline, oxygen and glucose circulating throughout their bloodstream, and rapid physical movements can help them burn some of it. Forcing them to sit still can exacerbate their feeling of being out of control and freak them out further.

3. Rebreathing will help reduce some of the oxygen in their blood. This is when you breathe in the CO_2 that you've just exhaled. Do this by making them exhale from their mouth into their cupped hands and breathe in that exhaled air through their nose. They can also use a paper bag to achieve the same effect. This will assist in dropping the heart rate and slowing the breathing. It also brings their attention to their breathing, which is meditative and helps pull focus away from the perceived threat.

4. Once safety is achieved and you're feeling confident enough, you can start looking for the trigger of the panic. If you ask the following questions in an interrogative way, you may trigger more panic and added frustration. Think of pouncing on a crab that's finally come out from under its rock. Come from a place of genuine care and that'll translate in your delivery.

You can try to do this during but my suggestion is to wait until the wave of panic has passed. This can take 10-30 minutes depending on the severity and the individual. Unless you're experienced in helping de-escalate panic attacks quickly, wait until the intensity has passed.

I've followed the above steps for myself when I've experienced panic attacks and when others have called me in a panic. It works every time. I once had a woman call me while she was taxiing on the runway at JFK airport in New York about to takeoff for a five-hour flight to Los Angeles. She was hyperventilating, panicked and in tears. She was overwhelmed and couldn't calm herself down, so she called me. We went through the above steps and within ninety seconds, she was calm, centred and smiling. She even laughed a little at one of my lame jokes at the end. The five-hour flight that followed was like any other five-hour window for her.

It continues to amaze me how quickly your physiology changes once the mind has been centred and balanced. Don't underestimate how much the body responds to the input of the mind through the nervous system. You're in more control than you might believe. Breathe and take note of just how powerful the mind and your perceptions are. These perceptions may just happen to tell the body when to respond.

Questions To Ask To Help Someone With Panic Attacks

- What happened just before you felt the panic kick in?
- Is someone making you feel trapped?
- Did someone do or say something that challenged you?
- Did you feel trapped by what they did?
- What did they do that made you feel so trapped? (To confirm that you've found the trigger, ask them if by talking about their perception they begin to feel panicked or anxious again. If yes, you've found the trigger. If no, start at the top again.)
- Where was your freedom in that same moment? (Now that you've found the trigger that 'trapped' them, look for the balance of freedom equal to the trap. Make sure it is equal and balanced.)
- When you get them to balance their perception, you'll know it. It'll seem like magic – they may even laugh or smile about it. They're not psychotic, they just balanced their perception and can see the complete picture of what actually happened. You'll know that you've balanced their perception when a wave of calm washes over them and the panic symptoms melt away.
- While doing the above, they might say things like, "There was no freedom. I can't see it. If freedom was there I wouldn't feel so trapped and panicked." Don't

let up. It makes you seem pushy and challenging to them, but keep in mind that you're going to help them get to that calm relieved state by doing this exercise. It's not personal, they're not attacking you, they're just overwhelmed and frustrated by how they feel.

4
YOUR RELATIONSHIPS

"Love is not a victory march."

JEFF BUCKLEY

GET A BETTER UNDERSTANDING OF LOVE

Here's a word that has such a wide variety of meanings and interpretations that it has become a language in and of itself. Almost. So many people have determined their own meaning of the word that it's bound to confuse everyone's interpretation of it.

I know I was confused about love for a long time. I didn't fully understand what it means to love. This was because I didn't know how to be loved. Or rather, I didn't understand what receiving love was. That's not to say that I wasn't loved as a child or teenager. I was surrounded by love, even in moments of pain, tension and anger.

Let me explain what I mean. Love, as I've come to define it in my own life, is not what you might think when it comes to love. I'm talking about love without conditions. The kind of love that, no matter what happens in your life, you can experience. See, you're probably used to having so many different conditions to how love should be given and received that you'll find a lot of what I have to say about love hard to accept.

When I refer to love with conditions, I mean that you love someone as long as they fulfil whatever your condition or expectation is. You love them only when they show you affection, support, happiness, defend you, give you what you want, etc. Or you love them as long as they don't piss you off, challenge you, avoid you, act selfishly, push you away, etc.

This kind of relationship, whether it's romantic or not, is shaped so idealistically and specifically to what you expect from the world that no one will ever fit the mould you've created. You might find that people get close and it may look promising for a little while but then before you know it, they disappoint you. Just like everyone else has at some point. So moving forward, you find it difficult to trust that others won't disappoint you and you fall into a cynical cycle of defensiveness. Put simply, you'll stop letting people in so close because you anticipate that they'll disappoint you in some way. Thus, helping you develop even more conditions to what is and isn't love according to you. Does any of this sound familiar to you? If not for you, I know you're thinking of someone else right now.

I'll also reiterate, this isn't exclusive to intimate relationships with partners. This happens in all facets of relationships between you and your parents, your siblings, extended family, friends, professional connections, bosses, colleagues and employees.

Ever had an affection for a boss who seemed to look out for you like a parent? Maybe a mentor who has taken you under their wing? A colleague who has treated you like a sibling? Or maybe a friend who knows more about you than your family? They're all relationships with the capacity for love to exist. I'll explain further.

Let's remove the icky, sappy association you might have with the word love. Love isn't kisses, flowers, hugs and getting cozy under the blanket on the couch. That's what the movies have conditioned you to think love is. You know the movie I'm talking about. It's a different movie for everyone but it's there for you. The story that you've been sold as to what love is, what being loved looks like and what it's like to love someone else. That's not what true love is. That's right, I bring you bad news. That's why you continue to buy into the stories in these movies. There's a part of you that wants to believe that the fantasy of infatuation, attraction and passion is what love is meant to look like and if you continue to return to it, like coming back to a textbook for answers, you'll find the piece of the story that you feel is missing in your life.

Quick side note, it's usually the romantic movies that tell the story of what love should look like to the romantic types. For the less romantic types, they'll usually buy into the love stories subliminally tied into action and adventure movies. Heroic servants, protectors, superheroes, isolated nomads and explorers. It's all the same undertone whether you're prepared to admit it to yourself or not.

Here's why. True love is appreciation and gratitude whether it's for yourself or for someone else. This means appreciating them for who they are as they are, no conditions. It's not a matter of 'I love you if...' or 'I love you when...'. It's simply 'I love you'. The whole you, all of your parts as one complete soul. The good, the bad, the ugly and the beautiful. Like I've mentioned before, all things within our nature are balanced.

You are within the laws of nature which means you contain this balance too. All your bad qualities are balanced out by good ones and vice versa.

To be able to truly love anyone, as I've defined it here, is to see them for who they truly are. All of their parts completing them as a whole. Seeing the truth of who they are and by extension appreciating them and experiencing gratitude for who they are, without ifs, whens or buts. No conditions.

To do the same for yourself makes you an easier person for others to love. By accepting and loving more parts of yourself you put down your baggage and become more accepting of others. Otherwise you're carrying around these judgements of yourself and projecting them onto others, who are just reflections of you and your unloved parts. The truth is that they're dying to be unconditionally loved as much as you are. They struggle as much as you do to love themselves without condition. Everyone deep down is looking to learn how to be loved and thus love others.

Personal example time. I ventured down the road of psychology, human behaviour and philosophy because I struggled to love myself. I did not like who I was, I didn't like who I was becoming and that made it hard to function in life with others. You can imagine that it made it hard for others to be in a relationship with me, family included. I had placed so many conditions on what was love-worthy that I made it impossible to love myself and anyone else. All while dying to be loved unconditionally. I, like you, just wanted to be loved and appreciated for who I was. I wanted to experience that warmth, that light, that lift that comes from receiving love in its purest form — unconditionally.

I know that no matter how confident, self-assured and strong you may be, you have a fundamental desire to be loved unconditionally. I know that you don't want all the conditions you've collected and associated with love. I know you want to be free of your conditions so you can love yourself as you are and love others for who they are.

The reason you're drawn to the superhero or the love story is that it's a part of you that you feel you don't possess and would require you being like them to be worthy of being loved by others. That you have to be heroic in some way to be loved and accepted by others. Or that maybe someday you'll come across someone by happenstance who you'll fall in love with, no effort required. These stories are all reflections of the same thing — everyone's desire to be loved and appreciated for who they are, no one more, no one less. It won't happen. Not as long as you search externally for it.

My wife is the one who taught this lesson to me most deeply. It was before we got engaged. I grew and developed personally but still struggled to love myself. There were things about myself I couldn't see as worthy of existence. I wanted her to love me more deeply than she did. I wanted her to accept and appreciate me as I was, but we would clash, struggling to understand each other and then more conditions around what was okay would come to the surface. The tension would build and then push us away from each other. I didn't understand her and she didn't understand me. We both had these conditions that were getting between us, making our relationship difficult. Then, I took a step that I didn't know I was capable of taking — I chose to love myself as I was and love her the same. No conditions, but simultaneously prepared to walk away from the relationship if it meant that it was the only way that we could live the lives we wanted for ourselves and still love ourselves.

What followed caught me off-guard. She set me free. She chose to love me unconditionally. She open-heartedly said to me that she loves me for all of what makes me who I am and was prepared to let me go if that meant that others (you) would receive what was inside of me to share. She loved me for me – no conditions. She was so detached from conditions that she was willing to end our relationship. Because we were able to love and appreciate who we were in that moment, without conditions and prerequisites, we were able to set a whole new foundation for our relationship moving forward.

This is true love. To see someone, anyone, completely for who they are, warts and all, and choose to love them despite what doesn't fit your mould. Actually, more so because they're challenging the mould you have; by being themselves, they're showing you that maybe this is the time for you to shatter that mould so you can love yourself more deeply. So you can see, accept and appreciate who you are as you are. No ifs, buts or onlys. The whole you – because you, dear reader, are worthy of a love you have yet to realise. You have in you everything you need to be loved. Nothing more, nothing less. You came into this world with all the prerequisites for being worthy of being loved, as you are.

How can I be so sure? Because you are me. I was looking for these words just as you've been. I was wanting to hear someone say the same to me. I found these words elsewhere. I found them through experience, through exploring, navigating and attempting to understand everything I've shared in these pages. The more I came to realise this truth for myself, the more I was able to help others, including you, with the same. You are made of the same stuff I am. You have a heart capable of giving and receiving love. That makes you worthy of love no matter the source.

That stuff of romance and heroism is passion. It's a choice to suffer in the name of acceptance. That's not true love. The word *passion* comes from the Latin word *passio* which means 'to suffer from'. These passions you experience throughout your life are only small glimpses of true love and gratitude, like a pendulum that swings through its centre as it extends to its extreme ends. True love is that centre point. Passion is everything else. The more you get to that centre point of love, the more capable you become of giving and receiving love, to yourself and to others.

The story you tell yourself about what makes you unworthy of being loved is false. That narrative, that illusion, is what is keeping you from experiencing love in its purest form — unconditional.

I'll leave you with something my late father taught me that later a mentor of mine reiterated.

Everyone is worthy of being loved including you. No matter what you've done or not done in life.

That's unconditional love. Make this your only condition for love and your whole life will fundamentally change. You will see yourself differently and therefore everyone around you.

So I ask you, my love-worthy reader, how generous can you be with your love?

"There is no hope without fear, and no fear without hope."

BENEDICT DE SPINOZA

GET COMFORTABLE WITH COMMITMENTS

Commitments come in many shapes and sizes, dressed differently for each person, and they make people behave in interesting ways. My personal experience with commitments was one of struggle, but the more I confronted what I didn't like about them the more I realised the valuable purpose they serve.

Everyone thinks of commitments differently. Some people see them as something that brings security, others see them as a trap. Whatever your stance is on commitments, you can be sure that there's a deep and personal meaning to why you feel the way you do about them.

The thing that is worth considering when you're worried about making a commitment is that it's not the commitment itself that you're feeling trapped by. It's the outcome.

Think of a commitment like a journey and the outcome as being the destination. You think you're scared of going on the journey but what you're really afraid of is arriving at the destination. When you consider re-framing a commitment this way, you come to understand how you're actually seeing it.

The reality is that everyone has commitment issues when they believe the destination is going to cause them some form of pain or discomfort.

Think about it. If you knew that driving down a certain road was going to cause you pain, would you commit to driving down the road in the first place? No. So does that make you a commitment-phobe, or just someone who is aware they're about to experience pain?

If you're someone who struggles with making and keeping commitments, then it's worth understanding that there are common traits to the commitments you struggle with.

Think about commitments you struggle with. Use one in the past if it helps, and think about what specifically you believed was going to happen if you followed through on your commitment.

A common place where commitment challenges show up is in relationships. People struggle to commit themselves to another person because the underlying belief is that if they choose to be in the relationship, they will endure pain in some form. Usually emotional pain.

It's common for people to anticipate some sense of betrayal when it comes to pain in a relationship. Time and time again, people will tell me how they're not quite ready to get back into a relationship because they don't want any commitments at the moment. When I question and dig through their beliefs, I quickly find that they hold a belief that they're going to be betrayed by a partner if they enter a relationship. So they don't get into one.

I get it, I'd be the same if I had the same belief. But when I start asking questions and suggest the idea that they weren't really betrayed in the first place, it stops being a belief they can hold onto. This immediately dissolves their fear of committing to a relationship and makes it easier for them to consciously choose how their romantic life unfolds. The fear, anxiety and panic of being trapped in a relationship dissipates and allows for the full potential of the relationship to flourish. It's a reframe. Instead of two people committing to each other, they're both committing to the relationship – the vessel that keeps them relating to one another.

Commitment issues are not limited to relationships though. They can exist in business or at work. They can even manifest as avoidance of travel and holidaying. Whatever the form of the fear, it's all the same thing. The commitment is the road to the painful destination. By changing your view of the destination, from one of fear to one of appreciation, you no longer fear the road you take.

Other times, you might be scared of committing yourself to a new job, starting a business or taking on a big client. What you might be worried about is that you don't have what it takes to deliver on what you promise. The solution here is two-fold:

1. Don't make a promise you can't deliver on, and
2. Give yourself the opportunity to find the resourcefulness within you to deliver.

Overcoming commitment issues is simple when you realise it's simply a fear. I've covered how to dissolve and overcome fears already in the chapter on fear (page 95). I will help you make sense of it in relation to commitment here.

When you're struggling to make a commitment, I want you to pay attention to what the worst-case scenario is that you're picturing in your mind. You picture a scene unfold if you choose to make the commitment. You see something happen that can cause you pain in the future. Define what that is, get clear on what you're seeing. It's going to help you understand where it all comes from.

That scene might be something like seeing a group of people rejecting you or judging you. It might be that you see someone intimidating you. You might see yourself being humiliated or maybe you see yourself being betrayed in some way and that leaves you feeling lonely. Whatever it is, you will see it in imaginative detail.

Now, as I mentioned in the chapter on fear (page 95), the scene that you're imagining in the future exists in your mind because you experienced it somewhere in the past. So find a moment in your memory, in your past, when you experienced the same thing. When you made some kind of commitment and then experienced the same pain that you're imagining will happen again in the future.

Now ask yourself how that experience helped you. Look for all the different ways in which that apparently painful experience was actually helping you in your life. When you come to realise that what you went through actually helped you learn something valuable, you won't see it as painful and you won't be able to fear it happening in the future.

Put simply, if you don't see the memory as painful you won't be scared of making a commitment to a similar destination. The journey isn't the problem, it's your perception of the destination. By changing your perception of that destination, you stop yourself from feeling scared to set off on the journey.

And in case you haven't yet realised, life is a big journey. It's the journey of a lifetime. The commitment of a lifetime. Whether you're aware of it or not, you've been committed to staying alive this whole time. So you can try to convince me that you're a commitment-phobe, but I know better. You're here, reading these words, so I know that you're capable of making a commitment. You might even be committed to avoiding commitments (which is still a commitment). Now it's time for you to realise where your commitment has been this whole time.

When you do, you'll get the freedom to consciously choose where you place your commitment moving forward. Sounds empowering, doesn't it? That's because it is.

Now, are you prepared to commit to the rest of your journey? I trust you are. You've got a wonderful journey ahead with many stops along the way.

"Your sacred space is where you can find yourself again and again."

JOSEPH CAMPBELL

SET BOUNDARIES WITHOUT THE GUILT

Boundaries come in many different forms. They have the power to make you feel safe in socially dense situations and also give you the breathing space to do the things that restore your energy.

Setting them can be tricky though. Striking a balance between doing what's important for your wellbeing without burning every bridge you have is difficult, but once you master it, you'll find it much easier to do consistently.

I'm not an overly social person. I don't thrive on being part of big social events. I prefer a quiet corner with a couple of people having a deep quality conversation or sharing a lengthy story about something personal. That's my version of a social scenario that's energising.

Going to big parties where there's a huge amount of social activity leaves me feeling heavily drained. The only times that hasn't been the case is during parties I've hosted, which were still considerably small in comparison to most parties.

Why does any of this matter? Because setting a boundary in these situations can be the difference between feeling anxious and drained or nourished and energised.

Here are two effective ways to set personal boundaries.

1. The mental and emotional boundary. This one is the most important because there's nothing physical about it. It's also the one I struggled with the most because I wanted everyone to like me. I strived to be the people-pleaser for a large portion of my life because I, like many others, believed that if I showed people the real me, they would reject me and maybe even humiliate me. So I would put a lot of my energy into trying to manage people's expectations of me, which was completely futile and exhausting. So much so that I would resent ever being around people because it was just way too draining to maintain.

   Managing other people's expectations is like hosting a dinner party and running around topping up everyone's glass of wine every time they take a sip. While everyone else gets a full glass of wine, you sacrifice your time and energy for them and miss out on the opportunity to be present and open with these people. Letting people determine how you behave is a dangerous habit to develop. You will be judged and condemned no matter what you do, so why not be your true self? If you're feeling vulnerable, be vulnerable. Feeling romantic? Be romantic. Feeling tired? Be tired. Instead of trying to keep up a facade in social situations, just be you and be present with how you're feeling. Use that feeling as a doorway to being present with the people around you.

The more you try to bullshit the people around you, the more likely they are to judge you. If you're not completely feeling like yourself, admit it. Don't try to change it and they'll respect you for being open and vulnerable. People, just like you appreciate and value honesty. They'll also be able to relate to you because you had the courage to tell them the truth. Wouldn't you respect someone if they were being open and honest with you instead of trying to be a poser? What you've also done is given them permission to be equally open and vulnerable with you.

2. The physical boundary. This is the one that involves every two-year-old's favourite word: 'No'. There's an incredible amount of emotion around this word whenever it's said. The word 'No' has so much power that it has dramatically affected economies. Do you want to come over for dinner? Can you stay back at work today? Can you come into the office on Saturday? Congratulations! You got the job, it pays $19 per hour. Would you like to start working with us? Can you come up on stage and share something with everyone? Will you make it to our wedding? Will you marry me? Would you like to come over to my office so we can discuss the payment options on our latest model? Will I see you again? Do you love me? Did the idea of saying *no* to any of these questions make you uncomfortable? That's because it involved you setting a personal boundary, which meant turning someone else's request down. Otherwise known as rejecting someone.

We're brought up to believe that being rejected and being the rejector is a bad thing. That by rejecting someone you're causing them some kind of emotional or psychological pain. But is that true? Let's take a closer look.

I've covered that everything in life is managed by an ongoing conservation of balance in the chapter on nature's balance (page 39). Opposites exist to keep each other in check. Positive and negative keep each other in balance. Shame keeps pride humble, pain goes hand-in-hand with pleasure, etc.

If you're focussed on the pain you're causing someone by saying *no* to whatever their request is, then you're creating guilt that you've got to deal with. The reason you experience guilt is that you believe you've caused someone a more negative experience than positive. But this contradicts nature's balance of positive and negative.

So instead of focussing on the pain you've caused someone, why not look at how you're helping them by saying no? Are you getting out of the way of being a distraction to them? Are you feeling like an energy sap and know that if you go to the social event, you'll just bring others down to your energy level? By turning down that job opportunity, are you making sure the company doesn't hire uninspired staff who will affect the team's performance? By turning down the marriage proposal, are you setting that person free to find requited love from someone who is more aligned with who they are?

The answers are there; you've just got to look for them. By rejecting someone, setting a boundary, saying no or simply turning away, you're helping them just as much as you're making things hard for them.

Also, if you think about it, feeling guilty is actually quite self-centred. Your guilt means you're more focussed on what *you* did to them instead of how you're helping that person or group of people. You're so focussed on yourself and how your actions are making you feel that you're blocking yourself from seeing how you're helping them by saying no.

Start setting boundaries and your internal self-worth will begin to rise. Give yourself what you need before meeting the needs of others.

A mentor of mine once told me, "If you've got the option between pissing someone else off or pissing yourself off, always pick someone else." As I continued my journey I realised the value of this light-hearted principle.

You have to go to bed and wake up with yourself every single day. If you're concerned about everyone else before yourself, your own soul will begin to turn against you to get you inwardly focussed again. Start doing things for yourself and you'll find that going to bed with the person you see in the mirror will become something to look forward to at the end of every day.

I'll leave you with one last thought on the subject of personal boundaries.

Think of a country that shares its borders with other countries. If it had no taxes or security checks at its borders, anyone would make themselves welcome. You'd get people from all walks of life taking advantage of the land, coming in with their baggage, leaving some things behind and taking off with something from the land. If there's no tax for entering or exiting, no security checks on the way in and the way out, this country will eventually be stripped of value and won't be able to sustain itself, which would lower its self-worth and perpetuate the problem.

But if this country set clear boundaries and made sure there was a fee (exchange) for coming in and leaving, and if travellers were being checked to see if they had anything valuable to bring into the country and were asked to pay when taking something valuable out of the country, then the self-worth of the country would increase.

The wealthy countries are valued for their self-respect. You will be valued for your self-respect too. You may be initially judged because you're beginning to do something that seems out-of-character, but you will ultimately be valued and appreciated for your self-respecting boundaries. Start respecting what you want and others will respect you too. You can't expect others to do something that you're not prepared to do for yourself.

You've convinced yourself that people won't pay a tax to connect with you. You won't ever find out if they're prepared to, if you don't place a tax on your time in the first place.

"Inside every large problem is a small problem struggling to get out."

ANONYMOUS

WORK THROUGH OTHER PEOPLE'S FEARS

There will come a time when you will need to shut up and listen. But the depth of your listening will require you to detach yourself from being personally invested in what you're hearing.

Everyone has fears. Everyone has worries and concerns. But not everyone is capable of listening to the fears and concerns of people close to them without trying to do something about it. That's right, I mean listening without fixing. Your ability to listen to the fears of someone without offering advice, without stepping in and fixing the issue for them, will be fundamental to the strength of your relationship.

Let's inspect this for a moment. Let's say your partner has a concern or worry that she doesn't know how to voice (change the genders if you like). She holds back her words while she watches you make a decision or take action on something. She's thinking, "If I say something, he's going to get defensive, he's going to try and change my mind, or just tell me there's nothing to worry about and dismiss my concerns altogether." So lips are sealed and fears concealed. Then eventually the proverbial shit hits the fan, arguments follow and it ends in, "Why didn't you tell me how you felt to begin with?" We've all heard that tune before.

Why does this happen? Two people in a relationship don't have the ability to communicate at the time when communication is crucial for all who are involved. For example – when it came to making the decision to leave my day job to pursue a career in changing people's lives, I had to have several conversations with my wife until I felt I actually understood her concerns about my decision.

I had made the decision to leave months before I acted on it. I couldn't find the right timing and waited for that moment to strike, but in the meantime, I had plans to work out and manage. Part of that was planning for how our relationship was going to be affected by my decision and how my wife was going to respond to the change.

We spoke endlessly on several occasions about how she felt about it, but I kept coming up against a wall when it came to a backup plan and what the worst-case scenario would look like. She'd struggle to get to the core of the matter and I felt myself get defensive whenever we reached the same part of the conversation. Then, things came to a head and it was time for me to decide how I was going to move forward in my life. That meant it was time for a gloves-off conversation with my wife. I knew going into this round that I had to approach it differently so we could get to a resolution.

So I did what I was used to doing. I asked questions and then listened. I asked difficult and personal questions. I just knew I had to ask. So I did. I asked, I waited for an answer and then asked another question. It was easy for me because I had done so much of it previously with her, but when I first started doing it early in our relationship, I struggled to stay quiet. In fact, there were times when I was literally biting the tip of my tongue behind closed lips just to control myself. It worked like magic. I kept quiet.

Here's the key to the magic of it. Don't take it personally. Don't try and take responsibility for the way they're feeling or thinking. That's not for you to control. What's important is that you create the space for honesty and candour. If taking things personally is your default response, you won't really give them the opportunity to open up without feeling judged.

By letting my wife speak, by giving her the space needed to be candid without worrying about my criticisms or defensiveness, she was able to tell me that she worried I'd do something financially reckless that would cause a big problem for us.

Being able to dig that out was relieving for her and for me because I finally got to the bottom of her concerns. When I asked her what I had done in the past which led her to believe I'd do it again, she told me with honesty. This made it incredibly clear for me to truly understand how she was seeing things and how that translated into her fears and concerns. By that point, it was almost impossible for me to be defensive or accuse her of being wrong because she was completely open with me. Being open with me about her concerns deepened the trust she had in me and our relationship. I showed her that she could trust me. It wasn't by convincing her that she could. It was by listening to her.

Trust is a powerful human experience. To develop trust in any relationship, whether personal or professional, requires openness and candour. You won't earn anyone's trust with words alone. You can do all the convincing in the world and they still won't trust you. Follow through with actions and that's where the trust forms. If you want someone to trust you with their vulnerability, you've got to be there when they're vulnerable and be prepared to be vulnerable yourself.

Think of the old trust test. You stand 3-4 feet behind your friend and tell them to fall back without moving their feet. All they have to do is fall as if they're going to land on a pile of soft pillows. The trick is they have to face forward the whole time and trust that you're going to catch them. If you haven't done this exercise before, it may take a huge amount of persuasion to convince your friend to fall back and trust you. You may even get frustrated that they're so reluctant to trust you in the first place, which can make you impatient. Your impatience registers as more reason for them to be concerned and not trust that you have their interests at heart. This could eventually lead to a forfeit in the exercise, leaving both of you walking away frustrated and disheartened.

Now, what if instead of convincing your friend, you opened up and admitted that you'd be concerned too if you had to be the person falling backwards? What if you simply said, "I get it, there's a risk of you hurting yourself. I have no reason to let you fall, but I understand if you want to walk away." They may still be reluctant, but they'll appreciate that you understand their concerns. They don't fully trust you yet.

But they still want to take the risk – because you chose to be vulnerable first – and so they let go and fall back. During those microseconds of free falling, they still don't trust you. It's not until the moment they feel you catching them (the result of your actions, not your words) that they develop a trust in you.

Now, back to the candid conversation. They don't fully trust you while they're opening up. The moment they trust you is when you choose to put them above your own ego and defensiveness. The moment you choose to ask another question instead of jumping into defending yourself or dismissing their concerns.

Putting your ego (pride) aside long enough to listen can be one of the most powerful things you can do in a relationship. Whether it's with your partner, your dearest friend, your boss, your assistant, your parents, your children or the person you're hiring.

You can get to know someone by asking about the things they love and the things that inspire them, but you can learn equally valuable, if not more valuable, things about them by understanding their fears and concerns. Everyone has fears, but not everyone shares them. By opening up about your own and creating a platform where you're trusted, your relationship will evolve and grow into a new chapter. That conversation starts with you, though. This leads me to ask the question: Are you prepared to listen to their fears even if they're about you?

"Move out or grow in any dimensions and pain as well as joy will be your reward. A full life will be full of pain. But the only alternative is not to live life fully or not to live at all."

M. SCOTT PECK

CONFRONT SOMEONE YOU'RE INTIMIDATED BY

A mentor of mine called me out on a belief I had verbalised one day. She said no one likes confrontation. People resist it as much as possible whether they're aware of it or not. I find this fascinating, especially as someone who has experienced various forms of conflict and confrontation throughout my life. It was easy for me to believe that people who acted like bullies actually got a thrill from confrontation.

Without side-stepping into tangents of psychological studies of criminals and murderers, let me be clear. I'm talking about confrontation. When two people disagree, don't like each other or feel as though the other person is getting in the way of their intentions.

I personally think confrontation to be valuable. I don't always like it and I certainly don't go looking for it, but if confrontation is necessary, I will do what I can to step up and deal with it the best way I know. I didn't always think and feel this way. I used to avoid conflict and, whenever possible, would attempt to correct or fix any differences in battle with people.

Here's the core of it. Confrontation usually happens when two people don't understand each other. When there's a misunderstanding, there's usually someone unnecessarily taking something personally. This leads to flared-up egos and circling arguments. A combination destined for battle.

There will come a time when you'll have to confront someone who intimidates you. This can be a difficult situation to navigate. How do you stand up to someone you believe has something greater than you? Someone who has a strength or power that you don't possess? Through leveraging the opposite.

Be prepared to be vulnerable. Be prepared to be open and honest. Usually, the opposite happens in confrontation. People tend to shut down, get defensive and step away from opening up. But if everyone is defensive, how will the conversation change?

By confronting someone you're intimidated by, you stand the chance of being rejected, condemned or even humiliated. Or do you? If you have the courage and the self-belief to stand up to someone you consider to be superior, the more likely outcome will be earned respect and seeing yourself on an equal playing field.

If you're going to stand up to the Titans, then you'd better be prepared to embody being a Titan yourself. When you realise that you are, you'll probably surprise yourself with what you can achieve and be even more surprised by the reaction you receive from those you're confronting.

At the centre of confrontation is the opportunity to stand up, value yourself and believe in your self-worth. It can seem like the opposite is happening while in the middle of conflict but the truth is that you're being pushed to value yourself.

Think of it this way. If you say something that may be in conflict with others and they just blatantly accept what you have to say, will you respect them or just see them as sheep who are too scared to stir the pot? You'll likely respect them for respecting themselves enough to say something to you. The same is true for the people you haven't stood up to because you've been too intimidated to say anything.

There are countless biographies of leaders in the world who have developed reputations for being narcissistic or, on some level, tyrannical, whose closest friends were people who at some point stood up and said: "I don't agree, that's not okay for me." It was their decision to value themselves enough to see themselves as an equal and share their opinion.

Doing so takes courage and self-worth, both of which you possess even if you don't believe it. Navigating a confrontation with someone you're intimidated by is a powerful way for you to experience that firsthand.

As much as it seems like the outside world determines your self-worth, that's just not true. You will be kicked, punched and hammered until you stand up, value yourself as an equal and say, "I believe in myself enough to stand up for what I believe in." Metaphorically, that is.

Anytime you find yourself avoiding conflict that you know will involve progress, keep in the back of your mind that you are avoiding an opportunity to grow and to value yourself.

Look back at any time in your past when you were stepping into a confrontation and you'll most likely find that it was your chance to step up and value yourself.

You don't have to look for a fight but if you're running away from a confrontation that will persist unless you step up, then it's time for you to rise to the occasion. It'll be worth it. You're worth it, aren't you?

Ultimately, it's not about the confrontation itself. It's about who you become in the process of stepping up. That's who you're meant to be.

“The great enemy of communication, we find, is the illusion of it.”

WILLIAM H. WHYTE

NAVIGATE AN ARGUMENT

This is treacherous territory, so step lightly. Arguments are a crucial part of relationships. That's because they require each partner to openly communicate. Any of you who deny this are living in an illusion when it comes to relationships.

Being in any kind of relationship will naturally surface disagreements and conflict. How you navigate these situations will have a vital impact on the survival of these relationships. Why? Because while an argument may seem to be an exchange of words based in anger, it's actually two people struggling to get vulnerable enough to openly express what they're really thinking and feeling.

Beneath the surface of each argument is the desire to be heard, understood and appreciated. However, if you're too scared to open up and be vulnerable, the argument will run endlessly exhausting both of you. Those are the arguments where you've both forgotten what you were initially arguing about. Somehow you ended up arguing about what *they* said about what *you* said in response to a comment that was made midway through the argument. It's a vicious circle of frustration and confusion that leads absolutely nowhere.

So, how do you open up and be vulnerable in such a hostile scenario? Using courage. You have it, you're just too scared to use it. One of you has to have the courage to step forward heart-on-sleeve and bare all that is on your mind. This isn't poker. In fact, it's the opposite of poker. This is one of those uncomfortable moments where you have to expose your softer, more easily bruised side. That's why courage is required. Show the hand you've been dealt. It's the only way you'll win.

You're probably thinking this can go one of two ways:

1. I lather up the necessary courage, speak my truth and share what's really bothering me, my fears, concerns and vulnerabilities, only to get shut down, humiliated and hurt.

2. I use the courage, open up and show them that I'm prepared to have the hard and scary conversation with them and I'm prepared to objectively listen to their concerns, fears and vulnerabilities in return.

In either scenario, you can't lose. The first one leads you to the clear understanding that they're not prepared to work out the conflict and that it would be wise for you to walk away if you can.

The second one will lead to a resolution that you're both comfortable with and you'll both have learnt something new about each other that can only strengthen your relationship or partnership.

As I've said, this takes a huge amount of courage. It means you've got to be willing to step out onto the ledge and deal with the consequences of being vulnerable – commonly known as 'going out on a limb'. If you're prepared to be completely vulnerable in a disagreement, then you leave the other person with no other option but to be vulnerable themselves. It's a check-mate chess move where you both come out winners.

This is the secret power hidden in every argument. Walk into it unarmed (being vulnerable) and you're disarming your opponent. You're taking the fight away from them and you disarm their ego. Think of a gunfight. If you drop your weapon, you're making it too easy for your opponent to win. They want you to fight to justify their anger. So to make themselves feel more comfortable with you choosing to be unarmed, they drop their weapon to make it an equal battle.

I'm sure you have your doubts about this method. However, this has worked for me in all of my arguments. Usually, we would get nowhere until I decided to go out on a limb, open up and be completely vulnerable. The whole dynamic would be locked in a stalemate of tension. No one could move. It wasn't until I took a different stance – vulnerable – that the web of tension collapsed and we were able to get to the core of the issue. Some of you may read vulnerable as being weak and that's understandable, because being vulnerable means psychologically stepping into your weakness. But I want you to know this. By stepping into your weakness you will find your strength. Avoiding your weaknesses only highlights them and further disempowers you.

If all else fails and being unarmed just won't do, walk away and reconsider your relationship. If your vulnerability isn't enough for them to be open, then it may be wise to allow your paths to seperate. This too will ultimately benefit you both, resulting in a win-win. It doesn't always feel that way but if it's not going to work, then it's not meant to be.

Another thing to look out for is defensive behaviour. That's caused by your ego and is typically followed by defensive body language – arms crossed, saying, "No, I didn't" and walking away. It may even include body language like turning your head to face another way. That's a pointless argument, it just flares up egos and perpetuates the anger.

So if that's not proper arguing, then what is? Arguing properly factors in one very important idea – arguing isn't about being right, it's about being heard. It's a two-way street. You're not the only one who needs to be heard, so does your opposition. This means for you to break the cycle, you'd best be prepared to listen objectively.

Understand that when you're arguing with someone it's rarely a personal attack on you and more so about them and the way they feel about something you've done or said. Meaning, it's how they've interpreted and perceived what you've done or not done, said or not said. So give them permission to have their own perspective. Doing that will help them drop the sword.

"Seek to understand, then to be understood." Steven Covey was famous for saying this. It disarms the person you're arguing with and makes them easier to approach.

The same applies to you – you believe that you're pissed off at them but the reality is that there's something internally bothering you. You perceive something has happened to you, even if it hasn't. It's just your perception, and your perception is keeping the argument locked where it is.

If you're getting stuck going in circles, then try to mediate your own argument. Listen to what you're saying as if you're someone else, and listen to the other person as if they're not talking about you. This is being objective. This can give you the perspective you need to get to the core of the problem to resolve the conflict. It'll help you see the whole situation differently and get to a resolution for both of you.

Here's another curveball for your arguments. Don't ever accept apologies. Apologies are never justified. No one has a moral high ground in an argument. Go and do your research on morals and ethics and you'll find they counterbalance and contradict each other, making it impossible to know who is 'right' and 'wrong'. In an argument, there is no right and wrong, there's only misunderstanding.

Either you haven't understood them or they haven't understood you. If someone apologises, then there's still a misunderstanding. Find what it is and get to the bottom of it. If they're saying sorry, it's because they still believe they did wrong by you and that you're right. This is the sign of an unresolved argument that will come up again in the future. Seek understanding.

If you truly understand each other, there's nothing to forgive. There's only gratitude because you came to a new understanding of each other that will help you grow together as a team.

I know how arrogant it can sound when I say there's nothing to forgive, but it's the truth. There's nothing to be ashamed of here. If you need help dealing with the shame, go read the chapter on dealing with pride (page 127).

There have been times when my wife has apologised to me because she did something or behaved in some way that I didn't agree with. I would quite bluntly throw it back at her and say, "I don't want an apology. I just want you to understand why I saw it that way." And then I would do what I could to explain my perspective as best as I could. By learning to understand my point of view or perspective, she was able to see why I didn't like it, which would enable her to do a very powerful thing – help me see with more clarity what my problem was with what she did.

By seeing my point of view, she'd be able to see how her actions can be interpreted differently, which enabled her to then show me her perspective on her behaviour. It would show me why she did what she did. Once we both get an understanding of each other's views, the problem resolves itself and there's no feeling of shame that deserves an apology. It's simply a misunderstanding.

It would give me an opportunity to see her behaviour differently and not make assumptions, ultimately allowing her to behave freely. No one wants to feel trapped in a relationship. Throughout our relationship, most of our arguments have typically ended with "Thank you" instead of an apology.

'Thank you' empowers both. 'Sorry' disempowers both by giving one an illusion of dominance and the other a sense of submission. No one truly wins there.

Keep in mind, while I'm writing all of this, I'm cool, calm and collected. In the heat of an argument, it's hard to stay cool. That's because your buttons are being pushed. Sometimes you need to say something out loud. Some things need to be said with a raised tone. Think about it. If you said all the same things in your argument but in a calm tone, you'd sound like a sociopath. Sometimes saying your truth out loud in an angry tone will help you blow the steam off the pressure cooker, so you can get to the nourishing soul food in the pot. Sometimes arguments serve as a necessary vessel to get there. Just watch out for the steam.

It's okay to argue, just make sure that if you are prepared to start an argument it's best to be aware of the responsibility that comes with the territory. That is, to open up and be vulnerable and share what's really going on beneath the surface. Anger is the bodyguard of fear and emotional pain. Open up about the fear and tell the bodyguard to go for a biscuit and tea while you strengthen your relationship.

Conflict starts as confusion and questions clear up confusion. Be objective, ask more questions and grow beyond your arguments. It's time to turn your arguments into a new form of communication. After all, the word communicate comes from the Latin word for 'shared'. So start sharing in your communications, it'll change your life. The truth is you'll learn more from your arguments than your agreements.

"If your heart is a volcano, how shall you expect flowers to bloom?"

KAHLIL GIBRAN

MAKE UP AFTER A FIGHT

This will get uncomfortable. That's because it can be an awkward and dangerous area. You and your opponent have likely just been hostile with each other. How do you come to like each other again after so much tension, disagreement and frustration?

It takes a degree of courage. Actually, it takes a lot of courage to do what's necessary to make up after a fight. Firstly, read the chapter on how to have an argument (page 245) to help you understand what comes next. The gist of it is that you're required to understand what your opponent was trying to communicate to you. It may have been hard for them to communicate clearly because anger, frustration, fear, shame and guilt were getting in the way of their message.

Getting to the bottom of what the issue is and understanding what they're trying to show you will make a world of difference to both of you as well as the outcome.

Being able to get to a place where you both understand each other naturally leads you to a place of gratitude. That's right, say thank you. That's the best way to dismantle a tense situation and help speed up the make-up process. Honestly thanking them for having the courage to tell you what was going through their mind and to share what they had to share with you can dampen the ignition wick.

This won't be the last time you have an argument or disagreement. It usually happens because something hasn't been said clearly or something hasn't been said for a long time while assumptions were left to fill in the blanks of the mind. Either way, another fight will show its face. So it's best to get comfortable with saying thank you when it's over. The more you're able to, the more you disarm the tension and allow it to dissipate.

By doing so, there's no room for discomfort and awkwardness. You'll create the room between you to get comfortable and open up with each other again. You'll probably find that you become closer for it and the relationship, whether professional or personal, will strengthen. Think that what was once a thread connecting the two of you is now a thicker and stronger rope. It'll take a sharper, more consistent edge to break it down and sever it. But it's unlikely to get that far next time because you've learnt more about each other through this.

Get to saying your 'thank you' and be specific why. You do so by saying, "Thank you for..." This forces you to be genuine about your gratitude. The more honest the gratitude, the more welcoming your recipient will be. It's impossible to be genuinely grateful and angry at the same time. Note the word *genuinely*. So picking gratitude will help you let go of the story that's driving the anger.

Keep in mind though, if you're forcing yourself to be grateful and you're sounding really robotic, condescending or dismissive, then you're not being honest and that's going to add more fuel to the fire. If you can smell bullshit from a mile away then so can everyone else. Save yourself the angst of having to navigate extra tension by being authentic with your gratitude. It speaks volumes about how much you care about them. Even when you're mad.

So, take a deep breath, find gratitude and share it with the person who just wants you to understand what they mean. Express your gratitude and they won't be able to do anything other than say thank you. Sounds fair, doesn't it? Yeah, I thought so too. Thanks.

"Love grants in a moment what toil can hardly achieve in an age."

JOHANN WOLFGANG VON GOETHE

TELL THEM THAT YOU LOVE THEM

Isn't love an interesting word? The word has such a strong aura and preconception. It can bring people in closer and push people away when it seems inappropriate. It has the power to deepen connections amongst family, loved ones and even friends. It can undo a world of pain that's been held onto for decades and can liberate people from a suffering that they endured alone. Love – the thing that connects us all.

For such a deep experience, an overused word seems inappropriate. It's an experience we all want to have, even those of us who are scared to exchange love. You want to, deep down. It's something that cannot be given without simultaneously being received. There's no debt with love. Not the love I'm talking about.

When you read or hear the word *love*, you may think of attraction, desire, infatuation, admiration, or more commonly, affection, adoration or even intimacy. I refer to none of these when I use the word love in this book. When I say love, I mean total and complete gratitude and appreciation without condition. Love without the small print.

Too often I've had people tell me they have at some point in their lives expressed their love for someone only for it to be unrequited. "They didn't hit the tennis ball back after I served. I showed them love but they didn't love me back."

I usually reply by suggesting that they had conditions on the love they expressed. They served up love with some level of expectation to get it back. There was hope, expectation, a waiting of some kind. That's not love. That's affection. That's showing someone affection and validation in hopes of getting it back. Because so many people confuse affection with love, they can't distinguish one from the other, leaving them to form false beliefs about how to get love.

What follows are things like defensive behaviour, fear of putting yourself out there, reluctance to wear your heart on your sleeve, fear of rejection and other acceptance and approval based validations.

True love, as mentioned in the chapter about true love vs. passion (page 211) is not something to be reciprocated just because it is expressed. People usually share their love when they receive it, because when it's true love (appreciation and gratitude) it has no strings attached. No conditions, no fine print. The experience of expressing this form of unconditional love is also the way you receive it. When it comes to true love, you receive the love back just by the act of giving it. Unconditional love is self-fulfilling and self-sustaining.

It's a perfect irony. By sharing the love you have, you receive it.

Visualise it like this. As you become deeply appreciative and grateful for the person you have this love for, the light inside of your heart starts to expand, like a star does. It expands slowly in all directions, in ways that can't be seen but only felt, for lack of a better description. So then when it comes to sharing the love, it can already be felt. When it comes to sharing or expressing this love, you channel that light through whatever means of external expression you choose to use, whether it's opening your mouth to form words or putting pen to paper to write.

The way you express this love may be in the form of a letter, an email, a card, or it might be in saying it to the person, taking someone's hand, touching their shoulder or hugging them for a moment. Whatever the gesture, whatever the medium, let that light guide you in the expression.

It will seem corny. It might even seem sappy or emotional. There's a reason why those sappy, corny lines in the movies work so well. It's universal. When someone experiences love, true love, it's contagious. It has a ripple effect beyond what you know. Believe me. I've seen the expression of true love transform people's lives, mine included.

If you want to express your love to someone, be prepared to do so without condition, without expectation, without the strings. Give it as a gift and let that be it. If it's genuine love, you won't feel the need to receive it in return. The act of giving it will be more than enough. If you don't agree then you're still placing an expectation on that love – which doesn't make it unconditional love.

If you want someone to love you for who you are – that is, without conditions – then be prepared to do so for others. Accept and appreciate them for who they are. I challenge you to find a more generous gift for someone to receive.

We all want to be loved for who we are. For all of our parts. For the good and the bad. The truth is you are worthy of being loved for who you are, as you are. That's something my dad taught me and later a close mentor. So imagine what you'd be capable of doing for yourself if you did it for others.

It takes courage to express unconditional love. It takes a certainty in knowing that it doesn't need to be repaid. It takes conviction to be able to hold space for yourself to express your love and to hold the same space for the unsuspecting recipient of your love.

Let me tell you though, there is nothing more powerful than expressing the deep-seated love, gratitude and appreciation you have for someone in your life. Expressing what you have inside to another person can do wonders for both of you, and dare I say, impact your physiology.

Give yourself the opportunity to change someone else's life by expressing your love for them. Tell them why you're grateful to have them in your life and watch the profound impact you'll have on them. When you do this, you're giving them a gift that can never be taken away, a gift that keeps on giving to both of you. Share a glimpse of that light and you'll be able to lift anyone out of whatever darkness they may be experiencing. Oh, and it's free.

If all else fails, try the twenty-second hug.

The Twenty-Second Hug

Here's a lesson, a gift, that my wife gave me. I came home from work one evening, turned on my notebook, logged-in, booted all my apps and with total despair, got ready to plug myself back in. My wife walked over, looked me dead in the eyes and without a word, gave me a hug.

She actually did more than that. She held me for over twenty seconds and it transported me from a world of struggle, discomfort and confusion to what can only be described as home.

Years ago I learned about the twenty-second hug and decided to give it a go. There's research[2] that's been done which proves that several hormones get released at a certain point during the twenty second hug, impacting your health and state of mind.

That's all well and good, but for me, it does something more important.

It gives me a refuge from the challenges and difficulties of life. It gets me to be present, silent and still. It makes it really hard to think about anything other than the warmth, soft touch and embrace of the person expressing genuine love. Find me something that does that in less than twenty seconds and I'm in.

That twenty-second hug was a long-time coming. It had been a while since our last one. Reason being I had been so caught up in navigating the challenges in my life that I had forgotten such a simple act.

She knew I needed something to make things melt away.

---

[2] https://journals.lww.com/psychosomaticmedicine/Abstract/2005/07000/Effects_of_Partner_Support_on_Resting_Oxytocin,.4.aspx

I was having a rough week and my wife knew exactly what to do. It softened my mind so much that tears welled up in my eyes.

Her one simple action cut through my crap and hit me square in the heart, reminding me I have one. So here's a prescription you can take to the bank.

Give someone a twenty-second hug. It doesn't have to be a partner, it can be your sibling, parent or close friend. It will be felt for days afterwards and can be the difference between having a bad day and one to be grateful for.

After all, what's life without gratitude and love?

"You can never cross the ocean unless you have the courage to lose sight of the shore."

CHRISTOPHER COLUMBUS

END A MEANINGFUL RELATIONSHIP

Here's a tender subject that can hit nerves you may be unaware of. It's treacherous waters to be navigating but unavoidable at times – essential even.

There comes a time in everyone's life when ending a relationship is necessary to move forward. Some relationships end naturally without directly saying anything. This is when people drift apart because life takes them to different places that creates space between them. Other times, bringing an end to a relationship requires a difficult and sometimes confrontational conversation. Either scenario can lead to an experience of grief and an inner conflict.

There can be several situations where the end of a relationship is required for everyone involved to grow, get closer to their objectives or simply live the life they want for themselves.

In the scenario where both parties are in mutual agreement, it can be easier to get through to the end. It takes little work to navigate this situation. It's mainly a matter of taking action on initiating the conversation. It can be hard to initiate the conversation but once started, it takes on a natural flow.

On the other hand, there are situations that require a difficult conversation that will go pear-shaped and turn into conflict, no matter how much you try to avoid it.

Those are the ones I want to address here. They require tact and strategy. They involve being open, honest and appreciative. This can be hard to manage in conflicting situations. How do you keep yourself open and appreciative when things turn hostile? By not taking it personally.

You're going to end it. That means you'll have to tell someone that things aren't working the way they once were or the way you intended. People tend to immediately take this personally. Sometimes it is, but a lot of the time it's not personal.

For example, if you sit down with your boss of six years and let them know that you're going to leave, you're likely to elicit a shock and defensiveness in the person you're parting from. Depending on the closeness of your relationship, it can get messy. You say that you want to move on for your own personal or professional reasons. They may interpret that as, "You don't like me, or the business and the role I've created for you. You're rejecting us."

Here's where things get tricky. The moment you start experiencing some form of guilt is when you'll come up with a plethora of excuses for your decision, none of which involve the truth. The reason this is happening is that you're worried that if you tell them the truth, you will cause them a large degree of pain. Let go of the guilt (page 119) before you have the conversation and you won't feel the need to defend your decision or lie about why you're ending it in the first place.

What you may not realise is that by ending things and leaving, you're actually giving *them* freedom as much as you are giving freedom to yourself. Let them and yourself go. You're both worthy of having what you want for yourselves, and if it's without each other then that's okay. Imagine a life where you spend your years holding on to someone (professionally or personally) for the sake of avoiding a difficult conversation. That is a life trapped by fear and I can tell you that your body will let you know that it's not okay with it. Not to mention all of the other areas that will be affected.

Think of the potential money you could've made by moving to a job you loved. Think of the people you could've let into your life. Think of the business you may have built because you gave yourself the time. Think of the time and energy you could've devoted to your body. Think of the marriage you could've avoided or the family you'd be able to start. The possibilities are endless for you. But as long as you're holding onto something that's no longer serving you the way you want, you won't be able to welcome in anything new.

More often than not, you'll be required to let go of something in order to let something else in. That's a risk that only you can weigh, but if you're holding on out of fear that what comes next won't be worth it, or if you're worried that what you're letting go of was meant for you, then you'll never move forward.

Think of a ship tied tightly to a port mooring. It's ready to set sail for the open seas but is scared to let go of the dock. Even though deep down it was made for the open ocean, it's so tightly tied to the dock that it'll never know what lies outside of the harbour.

Equally, the dock was made to see many ships come and go so it can fulfil its potential. By staying tied to the dock, the ship intercepts everyone's ability to progress forward.

Here's my personal example. I had a day job for years. The roles varied within the business but it was the same business. I left and returned twice. It was because I failed at the ventures I pursued when I left. So I returned to the nest that once fed and sheltered me. When I returned the second time, I said to myself it's only for a short while, so I can get myself off the ground again. That short while turned into years. It got to the point where inertia set in and the idea of leaving was too scary because of the amount of effort I would have to put in to make anything else work.

The trouble was, I was completely avoiding my potential. I was running from who I was and what I truly wanted for myself. I didn't have the self-belief to get myself moving, which coupled with my fear made it almost impossible to move. Inertia has its own momentum. That was until one day when there were a couple of interactions that made it clear that it was time to get things moving.

Without the gory details, I noticed that I had convinced myself that staying put while working on my other projects would be wise. I knew as long as I was holding onto the job, I wouldn't allow myself to receive anything else. The grip was so tight that I was unable to open my hand. There was no room for anything to come my way because I had my back turned on every other opportunity to make sure my grip on what was secure and safe was tight. Everything was telling me it's time to move on but my fears were keeping a firm hold.

Then I realised that it's time to end it. It's time to break up with my day job and start creating more of what I love – this book. No matter how much I tried to weasel my way out of having to take action, I knew it required some difficult conversations and that meant ending some relationships as I knew them too.

It's tough, but what's harder? Holding onto the way things are and stopping everyone from moving on? Or pushing through a moment of pain and challenge to create what's perfect for everyone? To help you answer that question, ask yourself, "What is this moment going to look like for me twenty to thirty years from now?" Will it be a moment you thank yourself for or will it be an opportunity you didn't want to take?

Give yourself permission to receive what you deserve and you'll receive it. If you continue to keep yourself in places and relationships that diminish your sense of self-worth, then you'll continue a cycle of challenge that will make creating change harder as more time passes. Let go, untie your mooring line and set sail. It doesn't feel like it now, but you'll thank yourself later on.

"When one door closes, another opens; but we often look so long and so regretfully upon the closed door that we do not see the one which has opened for us."

ALEXANDER GRAHAM BELL

DEAL WITH A TOUGH BREAKUP

Everyone deals with the end of a relationship differently. It can happen aggressively, awkwardly, begrudgingly, abruptly, dishearteningly or just coldly. Whatever direction it takes, the end of a relationship is typically emotional. Once again, this is something you won't learn to deal with until you experience it. You'll be taught multiplication and maybe even long division, but not how to deal with the division of a relationship. (Was that lame? Probably.)

Whatever the circumstances are for the breakup taking place, there are common trends that show up. At the core of all difficult breakups is typically some version of grief. It's not always directly connected to the length of the relationship but, the longer the relationship was, the more painful the grief. Or so it seems.

Be warned – I will sound cold throughout this chapter, but stay with me, I know what's at the other end of this bridge for you. You'll understand soon.

It's often the case that people see their companion as a void-filler. It's as if they fill in your empty spaces and your weaknesses and you do the same for them. This is why some people think opposites attract. Like two pieces of a jigsaw puzzle fitting together. While that seems romantic, sweet and endearing, there's an underlying problem with this idea.

The problem with people filling in each other's voids is that should the relationship end, it feels as though these voids or holes have been created again. When these holes are created in your life, you tend to experience grief. You experience a sense of loss. So naturally every time you're focussed on the fact that there seems to be a hole in your life, you experience the emotional pain of the breakup. Everyone deals with this pain differently and uses different patches to remedy the pain but they don't address the underlying issue – the codependence.

Let's take this a step further. Without a relationship, assuming you're comfortable within yourself, you will develop a dependence on yourself. This is independence sometimes known as inner-dependence. You will rely on yourself for what you need, also known as self-reliance. What's common for people who enter a relationship is they rely and depend on their partner for things that they can provide for themselves. These can be things like their company, comfort, affection, emotional support, a sense of protection, guidance, approval, acceptance and other variants of the same qualities.

When building a relationship with someone, you may be relying on your partner for these things as opposed to being self-reliant for the same qualities. So, when they eventually go and do something without you, whether it's something big like an overseas trip or something small like a dinner with some of their friends, you may struggle. That's because you're not standing tall in your own sense of self-reliance. You're not standing on your own two feet.

Now, you may be thinking that if you're completely self-reliant you won't need a partner or a relationship. That's simply not true. Stay with me here. I'll use the analogy of building a house to make my point.

Think of you and your partner as neighbouring blocks of land. As you build your house you decide to lay half of your foundations on their land and they do the same with you. It seems like a good idea at first. As you build your houses onto your own foundations you find that the overlap seems to make things stronger. But then your partner decides they want some different things for their house and they try to do things their way. This causes problems for you because half of your foundations are on their block. Naturally, this will weaken your house, make it feel like the ground isn't as stable as you thought and lead to insecure footings.

If each of you had laid your own foundations within the boundaries of your own block, you'd each have the freedom to build the way you want. If your partner decided to do something a bit differently, you wouldn't be so drastically affected because you've got your own foundations built within your own block to support your own house independently.

Building a relationship this way means you can share each other's yards (take down the fence between you), visit each other's homes, be there next to each other but still stand as independent dwellings. The sense of security, stability and simultaneous freedom comes from building on your own foundations. If your neighbour goes on a long vacation or decides to move somewhere else, you won't be as dramatically affected because while you were deeply connected, you were still independent of each other.

If you build on each other's land and foundations, should one of you decide to take off (end the relationship) the other will typically be left feeling devastated in ruins. This is because they took their foundations with them, which meant destroying half of yours. The thing is, you built your sense of self in them which made you dependent on them.

Here's a poem written by Khalil Gibran that is commonly read at wedding ceremonies as a reflection of what marriage is. It's beautiful, deep and succinct. But I feel that its meaning is overlooked by many readers.

On Marriage

> "You were born together, and together you shall be forevermore.
>
> You shall be together when the white wings of death scatter your days.
>
> Ay, you shall be together even in the silent memory of God.
>
> But let there be spaces in your togetherness,
>
> And let the winds of the heavens dance between you.
>
> Love one another, but make not a bond of love:
>
> Let it rather be a moving sea between the shores of your souls.
>
> Fill each other's cup but drink not from one cup.
>
> Give one another of your bread but eat not from the same loaf
>
> Sing and dance together and be joyous, but let each one of you be alone,

Even as the strings of a lute are alone though they quiver with the same music.

Give your hearts, but not into each other's keeping.
For only the hand of Life can contain your hearts.
And stand together yet not too near together:
For the pillars of the temple stand apart,
And the oak tree and the cypress grow not in each other's shadow."

The notion of two people coming together as individuals instead of merging into one will strengthen your self-reliance and independence. It will give you strength to be in a relationship with another as opposed to being reliant on them. Dealing with a break-up from a partner you were reliant on can trigger a lot of confusion and pain. It can also create emotional and physical symptoms.

Interestingly, a lot of the symptoms people feel during a breakup are the same as those experienced by people dealing with the death of someone close. Whether it's death of a loved one or death of a relationship, what you're experiencing is similar. It's the perception of loss. The perception that something is now missing.

What can also take place is a bitter sandwich of layered emotions. Anger, sadness, despair, depression, confusion and anxiety. They can all take hold during a breakup for a variety of reasons. It could be because of the terms of the breakup. Maybe they said they needed to go explore life for themselves or they felt like the relationship was weighing them down. Maybe they wanted to be single, maybe they found someone more interesting than you, maybe they didn't like the idea of being 'tied down' in a relationship, maybe they weren't ready to commit or maybe you weren't ready to commit. Maybe you were both arguing so frequently that it wasn't going to work out. Perhaps there was some degree of betrayal, mistrust or bullying in the relationship. Whatever the conditions, a dust storm gets kicked up during the unsettling time of a breakup.

For challenges on bullying, read my chapter addressing the issue (page 287). Bullying is the same whether in an intimate relationship or not.

If it's about betrayal or mistrust, then I best address that right here. This is going to sting a lot if you've experienced some betrayal. Especially if you're currently dealing with a breakup. I'm about to rub salt, alcohol and lemon in your open wound. Ready? While it seems like they betrayed you, they didn't. They were taking care of themselves. They were getting whatever they felt they needed for themselves. More specifically, they were going somewhere else to get what they weren't getting from you. In a more crude way, they kept going to the same grocery store for their favourite fruit. That grocery store stopped supplying the fruit they wanted. Instead of giving up on eating the fruit, which to them was nourishment, they decided to go searching other grocery stores to find that particular fruit. If the original grocery store had decided to continue to provide the fruit, it wouldn't have lost its customer.

The truth is that life around us is forever changing. The source of what you feel is missing is actually showing up somewhere else. If you perceive that your partner has stopped giving what you want (comfort, affection, protection, attention, company, etc.), you may start going to others for that more than you usually would. That could be colleagues, friends, family, pets or books. What seemed to be missing is now showing up somewhere else. What's more is that those who believe they were betrayed are unable to see that they were doing the same in other areas for the partner. They were also getting supplies (comfort, affection, protection, attention, company, etc.) from other stores too. They were shopping just as frequently at other stores for supplies that were just as important to them.

The harsh truth of it is that if you're unwilling to supply what your customer wants, then you'd best be prepared to see them shop somewhere else. After all, you've been going to different sources for what you want because you haven't wanted to give up what you feel nourishes you. That's why you were in the relationship to begin with, isn't it?

Relationships come with responsibility. The responsibility to build your foundation within yourself instead of building it within someone else. It requires you to be prepared to see that you both meet each other's supply and demand needs. It requires being as honest as possible with yourself so you can be honest with your partner. It also requires you to be open to learning more about yourself than you ever thought possible through one of your greatest teachers in life – your reflection.

You will learn a profound amount about yourself through experiencing the beginning and the end of any relationship you have. When you stop and think about it, what is a relationship? It is your ability to relate to another person. It is the way you relate to others that determines what kind of relationships you have. First and foremost, your ability to relate to others is determined by how well you relate to yourself.

You will learn to relate to yourself through a relationship and by being alone. Either way, build your house on your foundations. That way you can have guests visit, stay a long time or just pass through and you won't be so emotionally affected by it. In fact, the quality of the interactions will change because you're more stable and secure within yourself. Because you are standing on your own foundations.

"We too often forget that not only is there 'a soul of goodness in things evil,' but very generally also, a soul of truth in things erroneous."

HENRY SPENCER

DISARM YOUR ACCUSER, EVEN IF THEY'RE ANGRY

The victim and the victor. The lion and the sheep. Whatever the name, if you're playing the game of life like the rest of us, you'll most certainly come to a moment when you're attacked by others. This can take a variety of forms. I can't pretend to give you effective self-defence tactics when it comes to being physically attacked. There are plenty of others who have greater expertise in handling this kind of challenge. I'm talking about the verbal, mental or emotional attacks. It can be passive aggression, the silent treatment, being totally ignored, being avoided, or being directly attacked by someone who appears to be your opponent.

Whatever the tactic is that your opponent uses, it can work you up into a state where you stop thinking rationally and logically and begin to let your emotions take control. No one walks away from those situations feeling good. Maybe momentarily, but the feeling wears off pretty quickly and turns back into anger again. Then the cycle repeats over again whenever you get back into discussions with them. You'll default into being defensive simply because you're feeling like you're being attacked even when you're not. You're holding up a shield while no one else is wielding a sword.

Be warned, if you're fired up right now, you're not going to like what I have to say. It's as much their fault as it is yours. You are both equally responsible for where things went. You had a number of choices on how you responded to your attacker. The way you chose to respond is part of the reason why it ended where it has. So what do you do about it?

Whatever your attacker is doing, whatever behaviour they're demonstrating, they're actually teaching you something. I know you don't like the sound of that, but it's true. They're your teacher. Refer to the chapter on reflections (page 15) to help understand what I mean about that. I'll reiterate what I mean. They're showing you a side of you that you deem too ugly to bear. They're showing you firsthand what you look like at times. They're having the courage to express a part of you in a way you've been ashamed to own. In a very specific way, they're showing you that you're disowning another part of yourself.

If you're too willing to disown something you see in others, then by default, they have power over you. By behaving in a way that has you challenged, threatened or intimidated, they're pushing your buttons, which means they have power over you. The more they see that they're able to push your buttons and get a reaction, the more willing they become to push more of those buttons. It's just like that sibling who is so very willing to piss you off that if they see it's working, they'll continue to push. It's so effective that it continues to annoy you, piss you off, challenge you or make you uncomfortable even when hours, days or weeks have passed since the event and you're nowhere near them.

Imagine having the power to affect someone for days and weeks without being anywhere near them, without talking to them and by simply getting on with your life. Well, that's what they're doing. Their life has moved on, yet you're still being affected by them. So they continue to wield power over you without knowing it, simply because you have given them permission to have this power.

You want your power back. You deserve your power back, but you've got to do what's necessary to take your power back. You probably won't like what's involved but you're left with a choice: let them (the outside world) have power over you, or choose to take your power back and disarm the external world of this weapon. What is this weapon? It's your reflection. Your mirror, looking right back at you saying, "Can you see yourself or are you trying to convince yourself that this is not you?"

The single most powerful act that has helped me navigate the treacherous waters of conflict has been owning within myself what I see in my opponent to an equal degree. By looking at all the various ways I've been just like them towards people I care about and beyond, I can then fully own what I see. By doing this, I own more of who I am. They no longer get to own my behaviour for me. It becomes mine to bear with full integrity and ownership.

Why is that so disarming for them? Because firstly, by fully owning what you see in them, you can't be so easily pushed by their actions. The button they were pushing no longer causes a reaction in you, so their strategy has stopped working. Secondly, and maybe more importantly, when you own what you see in others, you're able to see what they see.

You're able to see their perspective, experience empathy and open your perception to see things that you weren't able to see from your defensive state. By seeing a completely different perspective, you're able to approach the tense dynamic between the both of you with a bird's eye view. An overview of the entire situation rather than just your end of the story. Importantly, this allows you to see their situation in context with your disagreement and come to a mutual agreement that works for both of you. It's an opportunity for you to be the wiser one and settle the dispute through the act of understanding – one of the most powerful tools you have as a human being.

The most direct route for you to get to a mindset of understanding is through ownership. Owning what you see in others within yourself. That way, *you* own you instead of *others* owning you through the power they have over you. When you come to own who you are, you become more of your complete self. By owning more of yourself, you step further into your power, which makes people who seem to be opponents drop their weapon because you no longer feel the need to carry your shield everywhere you go.

Picture walking into a gunfight with no weapon and no shield. You rob your opponent of the thrill of the fight. By making it too easy for them, you make it boring for them. By completely owning what they have within you, you're stepping up to their level and then choosing to not fight. You know you can match them if you need to but you choose not to. That's how you disarm your opponent.

The truth of it is that whenever you fully own your reflection, you totally change the dynamic. They change their behaviour and their approach to you without you having to do or say anything to them. It works like magic. But all magic requires practice and mastery. You have to put the work in and not just intellectually think about it. Do the work and get to the core of it. There'll be no arguing with your level of ownership and understanding when you can see you have what they have to the same degree that you see it in them.

When you're dealing with being attacked, what you're actually dealing with is another opportunity to grow. You're being pushed to own something about yourself you've been disowning and there's no mistake about the timing of it. Owning this particular button, this behaviour, this reflection will help you navigate your current challenges and progress on to your next step in life.

Ownership, responsibility and accountability are all yours at any moment. They'll help you take life into your own hands instead of handing off your power to others unfit and unworthy of the honour. If you let your reflection in others be your lessons to learn, they stop being the personal attacks you once labelled them to be. It's time to drop your shield, disarm your attacker and take back what's been yours all along. Can you see yourself when you look at them now?

"Everything can be taken from a man but one thing: the last of human freedoms—to choose one's attitude in any given set of circumstances, to choose one's own way."

VIKTOR E. FRANKL

RECLAIM YOUR POWER FROM A BULLY

Being bullied, confronted or intensely challenged can be a defining moment in your life. That is, how you respond to it can define the belief you have in yourself. How you define yourself has a ripple effect throughout your life in massive ways.

Take it from someone who defined himself as a victim for a long time. In fact, for most of my adult life, up until writing this, I believed that I was a victim of life's sinister game of roulette. Then I woke up and found out how wrong I was.

Be warned, some of you are going to get angry reading my thoughts on bullying. If that's you, great! Keep this in mind if you feel the need to put the book down whilst reading this. Your dislike for what I have written is your resistance to what you know is true and by putting the book down, you're giving up on yourself. Finish reading this, then you can hate me all you want. Just don't give up on yourself before that.

Let's be off with the band-aid then. If you've been bullied you most likely needed it. You needed to be woken up from your feeble daydreaming, from the fog of unfulfilment and quiet desperation. Take it from someone guilty of being that very person.

Time for a personal story.

I was fifteen and there I was, sitting dishevelled, dazed, and disorientated by my surroundings that were familiar only a few moments earlier. My ear was ringing, my cheeks and temples were screaming with pain and were beginning to swell. As I tried to move towards the ledge of the garden outside the school library, I felt a stinging behind my right shoulder.

I started to regain my hearing and my bearings as I heard the words, "Giorgio... Giorgio... Hey! Are you okay? Are you alright? What just happened?" A girl in the grade beneath me came running over as the dust was settling on the recent event. She wanted to see if I was okay and to make sure I wasn't alone. Swarms of students had come pouring out of their classrooms towards the fence while I was having my ass handed to me. They all walked past, staring at me like a deer in headlights, unsure if they should move out of the way or stand still to avoid colliding with the metaphorical car.

I was trembling with adrenaline. I could feel it in my veins as my heart rate and blood pressure were pushed to levels I hadn't known before. I sat there, turned to Marie-Anne to force out, "Yeah. I'm okay. I just need to call..." and pulled out my mobile phone to call Dad to see where he was. I pulled myself together enough to stand up and take three steps away from the garden I had just emerged from. I was immediately spotted by the help that came with Dad. They moved so quickly towards me they almost levitated, primed to teach my bullies a lesson – one of the helpers had a black belt in martial arts. When they got close enough to me, they noticed the damage and turned to go on a witch-hunt.

Dad was at the front gate of the school (where we were supposed to meet) and had made his way to find me moments afterwards. It was humiliating. My peers had watched me being overpowered, and now witnessed older men, who I saw as bigger and stronger than me, come to help me deal with my weakness. What was left of me was nothing more than self-defeat, shame and humiliation. That day turned out to be a rough day, but what I didn't realise at the time was that it had packed in many valuable lessons that would continue to have an impact on me for the rest of my life. And maybe your life too.

Up until that moment, school, particularly high school, had been difficult for me. I didn't like the way we were taught, and I didn't like being told what to study, especially by people who were being told what to teach (as opposed to picking subjects they loved teaching). Along with all of that, I had a hard time fitting in with my peers socially. I didn't know how to relate to them and ended up behaving in ways that were the only way I knew to be liked. Which was pretty much, being less of myself to be more liked by others. It was a challenge that I didn't know how to navigate. So I had decided the only way I could deal with it was to leave school. I wanted out. I wanted the freedom to pick what I learn and to explore the world through people and places. Guess what I ultimately created for myself?

I didn't see it at first, but I got exactly what I wanted out of the beating I endured. I got to leave school – prematurely.

And I got it with full consent from both of my parents and the schooling system. The following day I started full-time work and began my life earning an income. I was choosing the topics I wanted to learn and study. I'll come back to that later.

Let's get to the reason you're here – why are you being bullied?

There's something inside of you that you've been denying the existence of. Sometimes it requires a 'bully' to show up in your life for you to reach deep down and find that what you've been denying actually exists. What exactly am I talking about?

What happens when a bully shows up in your life? They intimidate you, overpower you, challenge you, confront you, threaten you, attempt to control you, and maybe even manipulate you. All of these things can be overwhelming if you're not informed on how to handle them. I wasn't informed and I didn't know how to handle them until later in my life. In fact, the day I started writing this chapter I had to confront someone who was playing the role of being a bully to me and my family.

Our bullies are here to teach us. They're helping us push past our internal boundaries into the depths of our character to find that we have a strength and resilience that would've otherwise gone unnoticed. It's like that shed in the backyard or the cupboard in the house that is the shadowed dumping ground of seemingly unimportant stuff. You never go in there unless you absolutely have to. You'd rather just forget about whatever is in there and you eventually come to a point where you're oblivious to the shed's existence. You become unconscious of it. That's where your bully is pushing you to go.

Go out the back, into the shed, kick open the door, fill the room with light and you'll discover that there are some incredible things in there. Those things are parts of your character, parts of you, that will help empower you to fill yourself with the resolve to be you, without compromise.

Here's what I mean. If you consider yourself kind, supportive, nurturing, helpful, considerate, sympathetic, affectionate, warm and compassionate, then you're most certainly going to believe that you don't embody the opposite qualities: uncaring, cruel, brutal, nasty, ruthless and harsh. Or more importantly, you wouldn't consider yourself to be someone who intimidates, overpowers, challenges, confronts, threatens, controls and manipulates others.

The problem with this kind of thinking is that you're denying half of who you are. Read the chapter on the balancing act that explains this in more depth (page 39). For now, it's important for you to understand, that no matter how you behave, there are people who will see you as a saint and others who see you as a sinner. That's because you are both and denying this reality is only going to make the truth have a more powerful sting later on.

What most 'victims' of bullying don't understand is that they're a bully as much as their predator is. You bully others as much as your bully does, you just don't see it yet. A big part of the purpose of your bully is to wake you up to the inner bully. They're here to help you see the part of you that intimidates, overpowers, challenges, confronts, threatens, controls and manipulates others.

To use the analogy of the shed in the backyard again, they're essentially coming into your yard, going through your shed and pulling out all of the things you've been hiding in there. The result is they are pissing you off. They're pressing on a nerve, seeing that it gets a reaction out of you and they're pressing deeper until you do something about it. They're pulling out all of your tools and stored boxes saying, "Hey, why don't you use any of this stuff? Are you embarrassed?" Mocking you until you own it. Until you can say, "Yes, that is my stuff. I don't need to hide it anymore because I'm not embarrassed by that stuff." Then, when it stops pressing on a nerve and they stop getting a reaction out of you, they get bored and find someone else that squirms under their influence.

Practically speaking, the way of not being reactive to their behaviour is by owning within yourself the behaviour you don't like in them. Are they threatening you? Where have you threatened others? Are they intimidating you? Where have you intimidated others? Are they controlling or humiliating you? Where have you controlled or humiliated others? And so on. Own what they're reflecting back at you until you can see that you and your teacher (what your bullies truly are) are the same.

It's also helpful to know what's going on for them. Here's what's happening for your teacher (your bully). They've got their own bully in their life. Someone who is doing all the same stuff to them that they're doing to you. Then they beat themselves up for being weak, vulnerable, controllable, timid, scared, an easy target, unable to defend themselves, etc. Because they judge themselves for being that way, whenever they see someone else who demonstrates the same characteristics, what they really see, whether they're conscious of it or not, is themselves and that hurts. Particularly, the parts of themselves they're beating up and judging so heavily. So what do they end up doing? They start using the easiest target they can find so that they can make the weak, vulnerable, timid person inside of them feel better.

Following me so far?

If you're a 'victim' (which you're not) then you're a reflection of the bully that they don't want to see. The irony here is that you're both reflecting the parts of each other that you don't like in yourselves. You're both each other's teachers without either of you realising it.

There were a few people involved in the story of the above beating. I had two people physically beating me while others were waiting in two cars near us. Just in case I was a master ninja that they weren't expecting – this was not a reality in my case. As I grew older and wised up, I realised that not only were these guys who were beating on me bullies in their own right, the real bully was the initiator of the whole scenario. It was a girl, a young woman, who I later found out had a crush on me. She didn't know how to tell me and used an argument we had as an opportunity to get my attention. It worked, she definitely got my attention, but not in the way she would've preferred. She just didn't know any better at the time.

Typically, people who play out the role of the bully are not only uncomfortable with their inner feelings, emotions and thoughts, they also don't know how to communicate them.

So they use strategies which look a lot like abuse, anger and what's commonly called bullying. Don't get me wrong. I'm not endorsing or suggesting that people go out and bully others. I'm telling you this so you get a clearer understanding of what's going on in the minds of those that intimidate you. Understanding transcends judgment, and gratitude transcends understanding.

So how do you disarm these people strutting around with anger and sometimes violence? You're not going to like the answer. The most effective way is to do the last thing you're thinking of doing. Own your inner bully. It's time for you to be honest with what you see in the mirror.

When you completely own what you see in your bully, you change the way you see yourself. You go from seeing them on a different level, to seeing them as being on the same level as you. This is important, not just in confrontational situations but also in situations with people you care about. When you see yourself as playing on the same level as the people you look up to, the relationship changes and the people you're dealing with treat you differently. They see you differently because you see yourself differently. You see yourself more holistically or completely – all parts of who you are.

In the case of being intimidated, if you're able to own your opponent (your teacher) more than they're able to own their inner victim, then they won't know how to deal with you and will usually go and find someone else that is an easier target for their unresolved emotions.

The aim here is to get you to be able to say, "Thank you" to your bully (teacher). You may be thinking, "Is this Giorgio mentally stable? He wants me to say thank you to my bully?" Yes, say thank you to your bully. As long as you're caught up in the story of the drama that you perpetuate in your mind, they're still controlling you, intimidating you and running your life. You're still giving them power by holding onto the victim/bully dynamic. They played their part, they fulfilled their role. Now it's up to you to step up on stage and play your role. Own it, see yourself as an equal and resolve your inner conflict so you can see that they were helping you own your power. Until you do that, they win. Until you own them within you, they own you. The choice is yours. You owe it to yourself to take your life back.

5

YOUR CALLING

"You don't have enough time to be both unhappy and mediocre."

SETH GODIN

FIND MEANING IN THE MUNDANE

At times, life can be a struggle. How do you find meaning and purpose in those moments of struggle? I'm not talking about the struggle with emotional or physical pain. I'm talking about the struggle with the mundane aspects of life. The things that seem to suck the colour out of the dream. Those grey, colourless, monotonous, soul-sucking moments. I know you've experienced them. No one in existence has ever escaped things that are mundane. Even the ultra-wealthy have to sit through some mundane meeting, exercise or conversation. How do you do it though? How do you find specks of colour throughout the greyness of life in those moments? Grab a paintbrush.

Whether it's something as small as vacuuming the apartment all the way through going to your day job. Whatever you find mundane or colourless can have meaning and purpose. Actually, it most definitely does have meaning. Nothing exists without purpose, otherwise, it would be unnecessary. So then knowing this, you're set with a starting point to paint some colour back in. Or rather, reveal the colour that's already there.

The truth is that whatever you're experiencing has meaning and purpose for you. You're being helped along your journey to get onto the path that you're here to fulfil. Some call that destiny or fate. Whatever your word for it, there's no denying that your purpose gives you meaning to live. A reason to live. The same is true for the small experiences you have and even the mundane aspects of life.

For example, you know all that driving you do to and from work? That's a prime place for you to practise mindfulness and exercise your ability to stay in the present moment. All without distracting yourself with endless thoughts about what you left behind at home or what you're going to do when you get to work. Maybe the same is true for when you're doing the laundry, cleaning or sitting on the bus.

How quickly do you get swept away in your analysis of life the moment you start something mundane? Have you noticed that you automatically slip into analysis and judgment of yourself or the world when you get a chance to do 'nothing'? This is why most people don't like complete silence and wrestle with the idea of doing nothing. This is why it takes getting physically ill for you to be pushed into doing nothing. But then first chance you get, you're up and at it again, even if you haven't fully recovered.

You know what? You're not as bad a person as you believe you are. You're not all that terrible to be alone with. You just rarely give yourself a chance. What if you were actually committed to finding a way to appreciate who you are? What would happen to those mundane, quiet, silent, lonely times? They wouldn't be so overbearing and deafening with noise. It would be you, someone you embrace, keeping you company. Not a bad situation, right?

The creation of this book has forced me into silence and loneliness a lot. Just me writing to you. But in order for me to be comfortable with writing to you, I had to first get comfortable with being with myself. It wasn't easy. It was met with great resistance and procrastination, which proved to me that it was going to be a valuable exercise. Sometimes, thinking of words to write and say can be a little mundane. Sitting down and coming up with words that follow each other in an order that can make some kind of sense to you has been mundane for me at times. Mostly, it has come from the heart, so the pain of constantly typing was offset by reaching out to you and having an impact on your life.

Between the waves of my typing, there's nothing. Silence and emptiness. This can easily be awkward and uncomfortable for me. I don't let it get uncomfortable because I want to hear the silence. This is the same experience people have when enduring the mundane aspects of life. People's tendency is to immediately distract themselves from this void of nothingness or numbness. But what if the greatest truths and lessons about who you are were waiting quietly in those moments of mundanity? What if your soul, your inner intuition, was calling out to you in those moments because it was the only moment quiet enough for you to hear it saying, "Remember me? I matter to you. I've been here with you the whole time." That's an important message for anyone to hear, no matter what walk of life you come from or are headed towards.

On the other hand, your mundanity may be helping you realise that there's more inside of you than you've been prepared to admit to yourself. Maybe your mundane life is pushing you so far into pain and discomfort that you'll take notice of this sense of purpose simmering away beneath your surface. Maybe you'll begin to realise that you were put here, in this role, in this life, to do more than only the mundane. That you were put here to make an impact on more than just your own life. That you have life inside of you worthy of sharing with others.

There is meaning hiding beneath the surface of your mundane life, whether that means getting comfortable with the whispers in the silent moments or realising that you're bigger than your fears, shame and guilt. There is meaning and purpose to be extracted from all things in life, even the mundane. Life has been mundane and uneventful for hundreds of years for millions of people before you. Yet, somehow they managed to find meaning and purpose beneath the surface of what seemed like a small life, a small existence.

Put simply, you can make life as mundane or as meaningful as you choose. It's entirely up to you. You get to choose. That is the premise of this entire book. The meal gets placed in front of you, but you get to choose if you eat it or not, how you eat it and in what order you eat it. You're not living as mundane a life as you think. But if at any stage you believe you are living a mundane life, you get to pick up the paintbrush that washes away the grey to reveal the colour hiding behind everything. Figuratively speaking, you're only as colour-blind as you want to be. The next time life starts getting mundane or you have a mundane moment, ask yourself, "How is this mundane thing enriching my life? How is it adding colour to an otherwise grey existence?"

Who knows, maybe you'll come to realise that you've been the paintbrush the whole time bringing colour to the world around you.

"He who has a Why in life can tolerate almost any How."

FRIEDRICH WILHELM NIETZSCHE

STAY ON PATH

Your journey through life will bring you head-on with a variety of challenges and distractions. It's probably even happening on a daily basis. You get pulled in a million different directions by all kinds of distractions in your life. It's easy to give into the distraction and let it sweep you away like a dried leaf being carried away by the autumn winds.

In the modern world, there's a lot of attention placed on how much you can keep yourself focussed, how much you can say yes to, and how much you can get done in your day. Very little attention is placed on how equally important it is for you to say no to things and minimise how many distractions you have in your life.

These distractions can take on a variety of shapes and forms. They can range from messages, bills and emails through to conversations, phone calls and thought tangents. All of these different things are pulling you away from your path. Some are more extreme than others, but they are there. The exercise and mastery of this comes in the form of finding your way to cull these things as they come up. They are simply distracting. They dis-track you away from your tracks or your path.

Make no mistake, you *will* venture off your path. That's important. You need to experience what detouring off your path looks and feels like in order for you to gain more certainty and clarity about what your true path is.

In case there's any confusion about what I mean by path, I'm referring to your mission in life. Following through and committing to your word on your mission and doing what you can to fulfil it. While all things ultimately help you work towards it, whether it's an obvious step in the direction you want or if it's a major detour that reminds you of what's important to you, it's all there to help you.

So then, how do you stay on your path? The best way is to stop. Stop for a moment and remind yourself why you're doing what you're doing. What's the purpose or meaning behind what you're doing? Does it align with you? Is it something that's fulfilling you or helping you get where you want to go? Or is it something that you're doing to fill the time and to avoid confronting something or someone? You might even be using it as an excuse to not address the shame or guilt you feel about some aspect of your life. Read the chapters on pride (page 127) and guilt (page 119) to understand how to shift those shackles. The reality is, the more important you make your life and mission, the more value you place on your time and your energy, and the more often you'll say no to things that are a distraction to you. As your self-worth increases, so too will your determination to minimise your distractions in all forms. It's hard, because it typically requires saying no to the things you usually say yes to and yes to the things you typically say no to. Either way, it's your choice to make, not anyone else's.

Just remember, when you start to veer off your road, stop and ask yourself why you are journeying down this road in the first place. If it's curiosity that is taking you away from what's important to you, then by all means, go for it. But if you're avoiding your road to begin with, then it might be worthwhile asking if that's the road you want to journey down at all.

Sometimes, the detour ends up being the path that was meant for us all along. Other times, the detour helps us find a deeper meaning behind the journey down our personal road and inspires us to stay on path. Either way, let those experiences teach you, and remember to stop every once in a while to reassess why you're going where you're going. It might just save you a whole lot of time, energy and heartbreak.

"I have yet to meet the person who ever regretted saying to the Divine, 'All yours'."

CAROLINE MYSS PH.D.

WELCOME FAILURE

Failure is something that is written, spoken and preached about in all parts of the world, in all languages and in relation to all things in life. It's an experience everyone has. It's universal to people in all cultures. People say you haven't done it right if you haven't failed at anything. But that doesn't really do justice to the experiences people endure when wrestling with failure.

The truth is that you can learn as much from success as you can from failure. It's just that most people ignore the lessons hiding in the shadow of success and become too bitter and resentful to see the lessons in their failures. So instead they walk away from these experiences feeling they weren't given a fair exchange for their efforts. As if life is indebted to them.

How does that do you any good? Sticking your head in the sand when life gets hard doesn't mean the experience goes away. It just means you can't see it. It's still there whether you're willing to look at it or not. I'm also here to tell you that there's no debt to be paid back to you.

Take my experience for example. After 'failing' at several different endeavours (including high school), I found myself coming to terms with the reality that I may have actually found my path. Being a teacher, mentor and coach seemed promising. I had life experiences which had taught me more than most people my age, and I had a 'natural' ability to help people completely change their perspective on whatever life was throwing at them. So I took the plunge and started a mindset coaching business.

I started participating more actively in personal development events, offering my services wherever I could. This led me to develop close relationships with leaders and expose myself to people I would usually be too intimidated to approach. While all of that was happening, I was breaking through my personal boundaries and developing a momentum I hadn't experienced before. People from all walks of life were seeking my help with their challenges and I was finally making an impact.

Things seemed to have lined up quite well. Then after making a couple of decisions that I believed I could handle, life took a turn. A hard left down a road that was riddled with potholes, cracks and unfinished construction. It was strange at first. I continued to move through the waves coming my way, but eventually got hit with one wave that kept me under long enough that I became disorientated and couldn't tell which way was up.

Not to worry! I had my life figured out. I kept moving forward doing what I knew to move through these challenges. However, no matter how hard I tried, I kept falling flat on my face. My business floundered, money was being spent on trying to bring life back into it, but it wasn't working. It wasn't just 'not working' it was failing. It eventually got to the point where I decided to shut my business down and seriously looked into other paths dramatically different to what I was doing. Maybe it wasn't the right fit for me. Maybe it wasn't what I was meant to be doing with myself. Maybe I only hit a short stride of success, otherwise known as luck. I went from being knee-deep in self-doubt to drowning in it.

So I spent the following twelve to eighteen months licking my wounds and deeply exploring what I wanted for myself. The reason for this was because no matter what I seemed to have tried, I couldn't breathe life back into my business. This led to a belief which initiated waves of panic, anxiety and depression. The ripple effect was far reaching and long lasting. Tensions grew in my marriage, I found it hard to be social at professional and personal events. I couldn't muster up the strength or congratulatory spirit when others showed signs of succeeding and progressing in their lives.

Basically, it was painful and led to a spiral of continuous failure, misguided decisions and despair that took me to places I hadn't yet visited in my psyche. The map of who I thought I was had dark corners in need of discovery. So I grabbed my compass and endeavoured to learn from my failures.

As I was pulling myself out of this trench, the realisation started to surface that instead of changing what I was doing – consulting, coaching and teaching – the problem was how I was doing it.

I was applying myself the same way everyone else in my industry was. I was trying to be like my mentors and peers. At the time, I believed that I was going to replicate the success these people had created. I was going to do what they did and achieve similar success. What ended up happening as an implied downside was that I subconsciously devalued my own style and approach to my life and business. I was resigning my own inner genius in favour of the people I looked up to. This is a sure way to successfully fail.

By attempting to be like everyone else, you relinquish your ability to express yourself and therefore fail at being like your idols and, more importantly, fail at being yourself. You will always fail at being anyone but you.

So how did I know that it was *how* I was doing things that was the problem and not *what* I was doing? Because no matter how many different avenues I considered taking instead of teaching and consulting, I continued to come back to the same truth – deep down, I wanted to teach people how to master their lives. I wanted to show people how to know who they are and give them the tools to work as a co-creator in their own lives, as opposed to living as an observer from the sideline of their own game. It seemed that I couldn't run from what was in my heart. No matter how much effort I was putting into doing the 'logical' and 'practical' things, this dream kept waking me, suggesting that it was not to be ignored. The more I ignored this lingering dream of what I truly wanted, the more symptoms presented in my body, the more difficult my external life became and the more restless I felt.

This led me to face the reality that it was how I was applying myself, not the destination, that was the problem. The vehicle and route I had taken weren't working for me. This is what my failure helped me see, amongst other things.

Failure is inevitable. It cannot be avoided. The more you attempt to avoid failure, the more you miss the lessons that hide within those experiences.

Your failures are actually opportunities for you to successfully get closer to the core of who you are and your path in life. The only reason you would see yourself as a failure is that you have failed to see how you were truly a success.

These past failures in my life were necessary for me to realise what I wanted for myself on a deeper level of certainty than ever before. The only way I truly failed was in my perspective and my self-judgment. The same is true for you. Your failure is in how you see yourself.

Think of the balance of contrasts that exists in life. Black and white, good and bad, dark and light, hot and cold, etc. How would you perceive and experience one without knowing what the other is? If darkness never existed how would you know what light is? If hot never existed how would you know what cold feels like in comparison? If you didn't know what failing, getting lost and being confused felt like, how would you know what success, finding yourself and gaining clarity is?

You need and will most certainly experience both success and failure throughout your life. Your journey along life's road is not smooth tarmac, wide lanes and cruise control. There are potholes, roadworks, dirt roads, detours and accidents along the way. You'll probably even crash into someone at some point. Just know that all of those obstacles are there to teach you things about yourself you wouldn't have learnt otherwise. Find as many moments of gratitude as you can along the way and they will be less of a nuisance and more of an enriching experience. That is where life's riches truly come from. You can't pay money for those lessons.

"People are like stained-glass windows. They sparkle and shine when the sun is out, but when the darkness sets in, their true beauty is revealed only if there is a light from within."

ELISABETH KÜBLER-ROSS

GIVE YOURSELF SPACE TO ADJUST COURSE

Life is filled with ebbs and flows in different forms. Times when you step out of your comfort zone and put yourself in the world, and other times when you step away and seek solitude.

Deciphering what to do from moment to moment can be tricky. But the more you practise, the more you'll learn what works best for you.

I want you to consider both scenarios though. There have been communities I've been part of where I've prospered from being actively present and showing up to events, conversations and opportunities. There have also been other times in the same groups where being present has worked against me.

There were a few times when I was beginning to notice that being in these situations was working against my intentions, yet I chose to ignore this observation and just put it down to having a bad day. However, the more I was putting myself in these situations, the more I began to notice that it wasn't just my emotional temperature, it was that I wasn't connecting with the experience anymore.

The same would happen with family at different times. When these opportunities presented themselves, I began to turn them down. It was conflicting for me at first because I was typically saying yes to these opportunities, but instead of forcing myself to go through something that was no longer a fit, I decided to stay away and focus on what I wanted to do (like write this book).

Stepping away, without becoming a hermit, can work in your favour. Not just for your own headspace, but also for how people appreciate you. Making your time scarce for others can increase their appreciation for the time they do have with you. You're changing quantity for quality.

Give yourself space from the things you believe you 'should' do and observe what opportunities present themselves. There are hundreds of stories where creative people go on a long hiatus from their field to go explore their lives and when they chose to step back in, they produce profound pieces of work.

So then, if you're in your hiatus, or only beginning in the world you've chosen to play in, how do you know when it's time to step up and shine?

It's more obvious than you may believe. You'll get cues from different sources that this is the moment for you to take the reins.

You'll get your cues just like stage performers receive when it's their line. Unlikely people will show appreciation for what you're doing. A variety of circumstances will line up to ensure that the opportunity is unmissable. If it makes you uncomfortable, then it's more important than ever to take the cue and step into the light at that moment. That discomfort is usually a fear, apprehension or concern that is based on an illusion that you're holding onto about yourself or others. Go to the chapter on dealing with fears (page 95) for more on that. If after that, you're still unsure about taking action, then there may be something about the opportunity which would be wise to negotiate.

On the other hand, be mindful that blind, fearless action can be quite reckless and bruise you into inaction, missing your cues and passing up on opportunities to prosper.

Watch out for those cues and listen to your intuition. It will know for sure whether this is the time. Take a breath and step forward. It's the best way to get through the fog of confusion.

“Success is a journey, not a destination. The doing is often more important than the outcome.”

ARTHUR ASHE

DEFINE WHAT SUCCESS MEANS TO YOU

Success is an ambiguous word that gets thrown around like confetti on a wedding day. But what does it actually mean to you? It's a word with a dictionary definition, but that's almost irrelevant because success is subjective.

To you, success might mean being able to fall pregnant or it might mean having a family of four children. It could mean being able to put your children through university to become whatever they choose. It may mean finding one person to build a relationship with, or someone else to start a business with. It could also mean reading one book from cover-to-cover or reading one thousand books. It may mean travelling with only a light backpack across a whole continent or living in one city halfway across the world for twelve months.

You'll notice that these examples are varied and are on different ends of their own scale. That's because success not only looks different to everyone but it changes over time for each person.

What most people do is associate their success with things. Typically material or possessive things. The problem with that is once those things are collected, they immediately stop feeling like a successful achievement. Just look at what you thought was successful five years ago compared to now. Or when you were fifteen versus twenty-five.

Try this instead of running after endless successes that leave you feeling empty when you get there.

Define what being successful looks like to you. Write it all out without any judgements. Go as big or as small as you want. Do it alone if you have to. Make that blank page your personal assistant and dump it all out. That page is purely interested in what you have to write and nothing else. It's not distracted by others or interested in hearing about anything more attractive. It's just you and that page.

Why is it important to you?

Then go through each one and ask yourself why getting that would make you a success in your eyes. Why do you want that? Is it because someone has led you to believe that having or getting that makes you a success or is it because you genuinely believe that it's what inspires you deep down? Be honest with yourself. You won't get far if you lie to yourself about what you want.

Next, ask yourself if getting this thing or achieving this goal is what will make you a success, or is it who you'll become in the process that will make you the success. Will achieving that success mean overcoming long-held fears, letting go of shame and believing in yourself?

Is it that your triumph will come from you giving yourself unapologetic permission to be yourself? Will you have to let go of beliefs that no longer serve you in order to do that?

Think of your success like clay. You can take it and shape it into whatever you choose. If you don't know what you want, you'll submit yourself to the version of success that gets marketed all over the media. It's hyperbolic garbage that is designed to get you to shut down what you truly want for yourself and buy into a deceptive fantasy that is unobtainable, especially by its very promoters. In other words, pursuing everyone else's idea of success is a guaranteed way to fail.

Follow your own light to what you define as success and by committing to doing just that, you've already succeeded.

Don't let everyone else get their hands on your clay. Don't let them influence the form of your dreams. You shape it, you mould it. Do everything you can to make it your sculpture. It only needs to be beautiful to you, no one else.

"True success originates from within, independent of external circumstances."

DR. DAVID R. HAWKINS, M.D., PH.D.

RECOGNISE YOURSELF AS A SUCCESS

I've had a lot of people who've come to me feeling disheartened by the results they've managed to pull from their personal and professional lives.

They feel as though they did everything they could to achieve the success they envisioned and still fell short. As a result, they beat themselves up, become fearful of making a mistake and carry around a cloud of shame wherever they go.

The only reason you'd want to hold onto that shame and pain is that you believe the sympathy you're getting from people around you outweighs the value of your success. Reread that!

For example...

In my first year of one of my businesses, things were slow. I wasn't making much money at all and I was feeling like a failure. As each day went on, I was struggling to get motivated enough to be creative or do research. After a few months, it began to turn into shame. What kind of a success was I if I couldn't prove that my business was a success itself? How could I help others become successful if I wasn't one in my own life?

Well, that was just me being blindsided by my own perception. I was successful, just not the way I realised I wanted. My relationships with my partner (now wife) and family were solid, even though they were challenging. I knew a lot of people who had fractured relationships with partners and family or both because of business decisions and personal reasons. My relationships with my wife and family were an important foundation for me at the time.

Having a solid family helps balance out the volatility that comes with starting your own business or going out and doing something new and uncertain. When I look back, I wouldn't change that. I needed that familial stability at the time. Without that, I wouldn't have stayed grounded. I would've floated away with my fantasies about how good my life was going to become as I became my own boss. I just didn't fully appreciate them at the time.

Where your success lies today may not be where you'd consciously like it to be, but I promise you this – your current success is showing up where you have subconsciously been wanting it to be. When you realise this, your self-worth will skyrocket because you will see that you are truly capable of co-creating the success you deserve.

You'll alleviate the self-defeating dialogue and become more appreciative of the work you've been putting in to get where you are today.

As long as you're comparing your success to someone else's, then you're essentially writing off all of the work you've put in to get where you are today. Making it all redundant and irrelevant. You end up destroying the sandcastle you built because you're comparing it to the kid down the beach who had a construction kit, form work and a slab of concrete.

So, stop and ask yourself where you're successful in your life right now. Is it your relationships, social life or money goals? Is it your career, home or family? Are your travelling to the places you've wanted to? It's there, it's just a matter of persistently looking.

You owe it to yourself to start appreciating the success that you have created in your life. Your sandcastle is special because you built it. Only you could've built that one. No one has your imagination and your creative spark.

Think of it this way. As long as you're comparing the current success you have to the ideal form of success in your mind, then it's like you're ignoring your current friend and comparing them to someone else's partner. Do that long enough and you'll be searching this book for how to deal with breakups because the person in your life got sick of the comparison and left.

Own your success. Appreciate it for what it is – your creation. Only then will you receive more to be grateful for.

"Do I not destroy my enemies when I make them my friends?"

ABRAHAM LINCOLN

TURN YOUR ENEMIES INTO FRIENDS

You'll have a variety of people come in and out of your life. Some will be friends, others will be enemies and many others will be neither. There'll even be those who start as friends and turn into enemies as life changes. This will happen. This is part of life and there's nothing you can do to change people's choices. But you can change how you see and relate to them in your life.

A person can appear to be an enemy when they oppose your intentions. When somebody steps in the way of where you're planning to go, they become your obstacle. Other times, their actions can appear to be an attack in some form. This is when things get interesting.

Your ability to navigate what seem to be attacks depends on your ability to not take things personally and your ability to fully realise what they're teaching you about yourself.

What I'm saying is, your so-called enemies are actually helping you learn something important about yourself.

There was this man I was consulting who ran into a situation with his employer that got him worked up and ready to walk out on the job, even though he wasn't quite financially prepared to do that. He was putting in a lot of energy to get work done both during and outside of work hours. He took pride in his work because he believed it was a reflection of him. For a while, before the situation unfolded, he had felt as though he was being undervalued by the people he worked for. This all came to a head when his employer told him it wasn't okay to log in and do work after hours or outside of his scheduled work days. (This was before the global pandemic pushed the world into remote working.)

You can imagine his initial reaction. On the surface he kept his cool, but inside he was boiling with anger because he saw this situation as his employer disrespecting, devaluing, rejecting and mistrusting him after years of service.

What was actually taking place was something much bigger. He was being shown by his employer that he would be more highly valued doing what he actually loves doing. He was being shown with great clarity the people who valued him more than his employers did, the people who valued his gift outside of his day job. Without this situation unfolding for this man, he wouldn't have come to realise with complete certainty that not only were the people he was working with not fully valuing his contribution, but there were people already present in his life who valued and appreciated him in more meaningful ways.

So does that make his employer an enemy or does that make him a friend? To a lot of people, it would seem he's an enemy. But to those of you wise enough to recognise the bigger picture, you will see this man was both. He was an enemy in one way and a friend in another. This event was a gift, as all events are.

By focussing on one small aspect of a person's behaviour, you trap yourself into a limited perspective. By forcing himself to find how his boss's actions were helping him, our pissed-off friend was able to see how his boss was being a true friend. His boss was indirectly saying, "Stop hiding behind your fear. It's time to go for it."

Find an appreciation for your enemies and they change their appearance. They become valuable contributors to your life and your journey, adding richness instead of apparent theft. Gratitude undresses all challenge to reveal opportunity hiding in plain sight.

"The fairest thing in nature, a flower, still has its roots in earth and manure."

D. H. LAWRENCE

OPEN UP TO PEOPLE YOU LOOK UP TO

We all have people we are intimidated by. They're people who seem to possess all of what we're missing within ourselves. They have their lives together. They have strength, courage and power; they're fearless, stoic and influential. Life is theirs to do what they will. Whatever the scale of your admiration, which is also intimidation, you will find it hard to be open and honest around these pedestal dwellers. You'll want to hide those parts of you that appear to be inferior to these individuals. You'll suppress the vulnerable, weak, scared, uncertain and soft parts of who you are in order to receive some form of approval.

We've all been there. And if you haven't been there, then you're not pushing yourself to grow. If you haven't placed yourself amongst people you're intimidated by, how will you ever get past the level of thinking, feeling and living that you're at now?

So what's the trick to being able to open up to these role models? Be prepared to be vulnerable. It's not easy, but the power of it speaks volumes about who you are and what you're prepared to do. (Read the chapter on accepting your weaknesses (page 71) for more detail on that.)

Let me paint an image for you. Imagine meeting the person you've idolised and looked up to for a large portion of your life. You finally get the chance to have a moment with them. You get an opportunity to share an experience. Once you get over whatever starstruck emotions you have, what's the likelihood that you open up and share a vulnerable part of who you are with them? Probably small.

You might share how long you've looked up to them. You might tell them how much you've tried to live your life like them, but you probably won't share something vulnerable about yourself because you'll want them to validate and approve of you. You'll want to come across composed and strong to avoid potential humiliation.

This scenario is easy to imagine. It happens frequently, especially with celebrities and leaders.

Now let's flip the roles around. You're the influential person meeting a fan or follower. Your fan comes to you and all they do is tell you how much they look up to you. They tell you that their first tattoo was of your face on their shoulder because of what you represent to them. Their firstborn child will be named after you even if they're the opposite sex. And all they want you to know is how much that thing you did that got released into the world shaped their childhood or teenage years. I'm intentionally over-exaggerating here. However, this is what a lot of people do.

As the role model in this scenario, wouldn't you be more touched by someone presenting themselves as an equal and being open with you? Wouldn't you respect and appreciate the person you're standing with because, instead of minimising themselves, they stood comfortably within themselves and opened up with you on a meaningful level?

Perhaps some more detail will help my point. If you have the strength to be open and vulnerable without being paralysed by your fear of judgment, then you're likely to be able to stand within the boundaries of who you are and not be concerned with how others will receive you. If you're the one leading the way with vulnerability and openness, you immediately create the space for others to give themselves permission to do the same. By leading the way within yourself, you lead your idols into doing the same. The reality is, that they're as concerned about being open and potentially disappointing you as you are concerned about disappointing them for the same reason.

If they have someone telling them how much they're adored and admired, they're being put on a high pedestal that creates a potentially long fall to the ground. So to keep themselves from falling so hard, they hide who they really are behind niceties and politeness. By being open, honest and vulnerable with them, you safely help them down from the pedestal which makes them respect you more so than others.

The truth is that you're worth admiring as much as they are. The moment you realise this to be true, you can humble yourself to all of your strengths and weaknesses and have a level-hearted conversation with the people you look up to. They were and are like you and they appreciate anyone who doesn't pretend to be something they're not. Put simply, authenticity is mutually appreciated and remarkable.

Spending your life only looking up to the people you admire will give you a sore neck. See them for who they truly are – people with hearts and minds, just like you. Who knows what may come of a single interaction like that?

"Don't judge each day by the harvest you reap but by the seeds that you plant."

ROBERT LOUIS STEVENSON

BRAINSTORM IDEAS WITH OTHERS EFFECTIVELY

Life can be lived alone. It can be done in isolation. It may be a struggle but it's achievable. The thing about complete isolation is the inability to learn from others. All your lessons and understandings will come from your own experience. You don't get to learn from others' successes and mistakes. Incidentally, learning from others as a collective society, group, community and family is what has progressed humanity forward.

You may live alone and like it, but a lot of your world has been shaped by groups of people coming together to make decisions through agreements and disagreements. Even if you spend your days alone, you may be reading books, articles and teachings from other authors that reveal to you something you may not have learned by your own doing. You may be buying products, foods or even services, all of which have been created and produced through collective effort. Whatever it is in your life you're currently dealing with, there have been people coming together to brainstorm, create, learn and produce to bring it to you.

For some, the idea of brainstorming and thinking creatively as a group (more than one person) can be challenging. Especially for you control freaks out there. Rest assured, there is a way and we will find it together.

I like the word brainstorm. It signifies the unsettled feelings that come with creativity. It suggests that things will get uncomfortable, uncertain and unclear for a while but inherently serve a purpose. There's lightning, rain and wind, and these are the kind of conditions that allow for unusual behaviour. Whatever the reason for the brainstorming session, there are a few ideas that can help facilitate the exercise towards an ultimate solution.

I'll start with the most important one. Whenever you're working with others, having the space to be objective, non-judgemental and candid allows for a seriously productive conversation to take place. Ed Catmull describes this as candour. I call it being unbiased and objective. Basically, it means to get your own personal feelings, emotions and perceptions out of the way long enough to see the subject differently.

This is important because if you're tainting your view with your own judgment, then you're not allowing yourself to see other possibilities for where things can go. Your way may be the most valuable way or it could be the way that leads to ruin. Either way, you won't know unless you're able to see objectively. You won't be able to see the subject as it is until you let go of your way.

As a side note, the same is true in the world of finance. The world's wealthy leaders have gotten to where they are by being as objective as they can about the choices they make.

They set aside their emotions and feelings to allow the truth to come to the surface. By doing so, they're able to see if a company is actually worth investing in or not. They'll even go as far as choosing to avoid investing in a company everyone else is profiting from because they don't know enough about its category and don't want to pretend like they're going to be able to educate themselves enough to make a wise decision. They let go of their pride. This also comes from being objective.

This allows you to detach yourself from the subject long enough to see it as something other than being an extension of you. Hence, being objective as opposed to subjective.

When it comes to the conversations and dialogues you have with others about your brainstorming topic, being objective with their thoughts, feelings and emotions about the subject will also help nurture the exercise. Not everyone involved can handle being objective. It's probably going to be really difficult at first if you're not used to it. It pays off though, so be sure to practise it as often as you can when it comes to projects.

Here's a strange but helpful example. When furnishing your home or office with indoor plants, you may have an opinion about where to place them to make the room feel a certain way. Your roommate (romantic or otherwise) may feel differently about the decision. Both opinions matter, and you may both get into a disagreement because you're being subjective (personal) about it. However, if the plant dies in either of those places that the two of you are arguing over, then these opinions of yours are negated. Effective brainstorming factors in *all* options and possibilities. In this case, even the plant's opinion.

Sometimes brainstorming has to happen around topics that everyone is avoiding. Things like managing the household budget, cleaning duties, hiring a caretaker, rehabilitating a loved-one, handling the estate of someone who has passed, applying for a new job or taking legal action. The same thing is required for both the avoided subjects and the exciting ones.

The best way to enter those sessions is for everyone to mutually agree that no-one wants to be there discussing and deciding (brainstorming) the issue. This immediately takes some of the tension out of the issue by placing everyone in the same boat as opposed to competing boats on the same body of water. Be honest with yourself and everyone involved. It'll make moving through all options, possibilities and opportunities an eventually smooth experience.

If at any stage in any brainstorming scenario, you notice that you're the only one being objective, own it. Don't try and force others into objectivity. Don't get up on your high horse and look down on your compadres as though they're inferior for their subjectivity. This attitude will lead the whole situation to a standstill. No solution will come of this other than flared-up egos and bruised pride. This situation of you being the only objective one requires you to lead through your objectivity. Hold space for everyone's opinions, feelings and perceptions. By holding this space, you give the subject a fighting chance to get through the storm. Resolution is the destination here, not admiration.

I'll use another analogy to paint my point. Think of a ship sailing through a (brain)storm. The captain, if wise, will factor in everyone's opinions. They'll consider all fears, anxieties, brutal honesties and possibilities. Whatever comes up is considered important, but if it's not wise, doesn't make sense, doesn't lead to a solution or goes against the intentions of the outcome, then it won't get acted on. If the crew with all of its differing opinions tried to steer the ship the way they wanted, the ship would not move or it would split into pieces.

In brainstorming, everything is on the table. That's the point. But by the end of the brainstorming session, the table must be cleared of everything that doesn't get actioned. It must happen without insult and without being taken personally. With our kind of brainstorming, choosing to not go ahead with an option is not personal. The same is true when going ahead with someone else's option. It's not an insult. It's about helping the subject of the brainstorm to progress forward.

Brainstorming is bigger than everyone involved. It's a collective effort of creativity, risk management, prophecy, perspective and inspiration. It's a dance. Everyone is listening to the same song but everyone has different dance moves. Respect everyone's choice to dance the way they do and who knows, you may very well find yourself dancing until a ripe old age with some pretty respectable dance-partners. So the next time you find yourself in a brainstorm, will you dance through the storm?

“Wise men don’t need advice. Fools won’t take it.”

BENJAMIN FRANKLIN

PICK MENTORS TO LEARN FROM

Mentors are an invaluable aspect of life. Mentors come in various shapes, sizes, outfits and forms. Sometimes they take the form of a teacher, a tutor or a lecturer. Other times they look a lot like your parents or guardians. Then at other times, they take the more direct form of being a mentor specifically helping you with an aspect of your life.

There's a principle that suggests you're directly influenced by the average of the closest people to you. You may be spending a lot of social time with people who share similar views on life. You may spend a lot of time with family members who you regularly disagree with, or maybe you have a variety of mentors who challenge you to think differently or encourage you to stick to the train of thought you're currently on. Whoever they are, you're likely to be heavily influenced by these people.

Some of my mentors have been in the form of authors of books. Every time I return to their books or my notes on their books, I end up spending a lot of time with them. French philosopher René Descartes says it's "like a conversation with the finest minds of past centuries." Authors of the past have played a big role this way in my life.

Small sidebar – as I wrote in the preface, my childhood bedroom was also used to store a lot of stuff because I didn't take up a whole lot of the space in that room. My parents had shelves drilled into the walls to store a lot of the books we had in the house. There was also a stand-alone bookshelf in the dormant fireplace that was in my room. I was surrounded by and submerged amongst many authors. And I loved it. They kept me company when I had bad dreams or when I was feeling particularly lonely. I wasn't the greatest reader – I didn't read my first novel cover to cover until I was thirteen and it took me over six months to finish. It wasn't until I was sixteen that I started to get more heavily into books. Either way, the authors of the books and the encyclopaedias proved to be mentors. They encouraged my curiosity about the world. Then as I grew older and dove into the more complicated subjects (like human behaviour) I kept drinking from the fountain of knowledge without having to try and connect with these people in person. There I was in a small family home in Sydney reading books written by some of the most knowledgeable people in their fields from halfway across the world or from centuries before my time. I got to have meaningful conversations with them on topics they loved and I got to take my time with the pace at which I took it in. I would take a bite of knowledge, chew on it a little bit, chew a little bit more, then digest it. Each book, each topic, was assimilated and integrated, like having someone show me something they discovered on their journey. It was a valuable process.

The same is true for you. To attempt to explore your life and your journey completely alone would mean to learn what's already been learnt. There's nothing wrong with doing this, but my thoughts are that it's not efficient. Especially as technology advances and develops, we are able to learn from what has been discovered, what has been achieved and what failures have occurred.

This is what defines a mentor. It's a relationship you'll have with many different people at many different stages in your life who can help you navigate places they've previously ventured into and learnt from. The value of having a mentor comes from being able to learn the lessons they learnt without having to do exactly everything they did. You get to learn by having them point out where the traps and downfalls are, but also where there may be some hidden treasure to keep you going.

So why would you want to venture down a path others have already been on? To discover your own path. This is a natural part of your growth, development and awakening. You venture, trek and explore, but for a lot of where you're going there are already beaten paths. Others have done part of it for you. Others have made their way through the jungle and have cleared a path for you to follow. This will speed up the journey for you. But you will inevitably come to the point where others haven't yet been. You will reach the boundary of previous adventurers and come to the end point of their experience. This is where you take the step and use your trepidation to move you beyond what you thought you could do.

Keep in mind, mentors can help you here too. They did the same at some point. They reached the boundaries of their mentor's experience and then took steps beyond what was already known. They took steps into the unknown. So this equips them with the knowledge and wisdom of what it takes to navigate uncharted territory. They'll help you overcome your fears, your imagination, your guilt about what you're leaving behind, your anxiety about possibly discovering nothing and even your desire to give in and head home. They navigated similar experiences on their own journeys, even if it was to a different place to yours.

Here's my point. You won't ever have just one mentor. You will have many. So picking one now is just a matter of working out what you want to achieve, where you want to go, what you want to explore, and then finding someone who's navigated similar waters.

Here are a couple of things to note on the picking process.

1. You may be unsure of what you want to do. So using that as your decision-making guideline for finding a mentor won't work for you. Instead, see if you can find someone who has navigated the same sense of feeling lost and confused in their past. There are more such people than you think, including me.

2. Sometimes you'll be mentored on something that seems to be very specific, but you'll find it relates to a lot of the various areas of your life. For example, you might decide you want to become a professional chef. The person you end up working for becomes your mentor by default. But the most valuable thing you end up taking away from that relationship is their philosophy on life and very little about how to be a chef. This also happened to me. Not as a chef but as

an electronics technician and the lessons were coming from my mentor, my dad.

3. You can't screw up the choosing process. I know it seems counterintuitive, but if you pick someone to help you and they turn out to be contrastingly different to you and where you want to be, then you'll extract deep value from that too. You'll learn something about making mistakes (read that chapter on mistakes (page 81). You'll learn what it takes to be clear about what you'd like from them (the art of communication). Or you'll learn that you know a lot already about what you were hoping to learn from them. Also a valuable lesson. You can't screw this up even though you think you can.

Now, assuming you aren't connecting to your mentor through a book, audiobook or recording, a video or any other media format, we'd best address the process of asking.

It's going to be a forward and somewhat vulnerable ask. You are asking for their help after all. You're admitting to them that you know less than they do and that means letting go of your pride (page 127). You'll be saying to the person you believe may have superior knowledge, that they know more than you.

So word your request for help in a humble but not self-demeaning way. Be prepared to be vulnerable and open without being self-deprecating. Even though it seems like you're only really taking from them, you're also giving them an opportunity to teach, educate and impart knowledge. Irrespective of whether or not you're paying them for the mentoring, you're still giving them that opportunity and if they're humble teachers, they know they're going to learn something from you too. All wise teachers know this. Like some parents who admit it publicly or not, learn as much from their children as they teach them. In this case, you're not forced into who your mentors are like we are with our parents.

You get to choose now. So ask yourself what you'd like to know more about now. Look at what might help you based on where you are and where you're going. Find a mentor to bridge that gap and let yourself be guided by their experience. You'll be guided to your next mentor by other people, by serendipity or by synchronicity.

Go learn, absorb and explore. What comes of it will never be taken away from you so you'll be richer for it either way.

After all, as the ancient proverb goes, "When the student is ready, the master appears."

"Experience is not what happens to a man; it is what a man does with what happens to him."

ALDOUS HUXLEY

BECOME A ROLE MODEL FOR YOURSELF

I bet no one told you it was possible to be your own role model. That you could be the gauge or the measuring tape that you use to live by. Well, I'm telling you it is possible. No, it's vital that you are your own yardstick. That you measure yourself against yourself and no one else. It's hard to do. Actually, hard is not a strong enough word. It's onerous and painful. Which is why so many people don't do it.

The easy thing to do in life is to find people you look up to. Research as much about them as you can and do everything in your power to think and act like them to get the same results in life as they do. Easy, right? Copy, replicate, imitate. Surely that's going to work for everyone. On closer inspection, maybe not.

Up until my early twenties, I spent a lot of time replicating the actions and thinking of people I looked up to. These were people I personally knew and also people I learned about through media, books, movies, and word-of-mouth. I believed that if I could live life the way they had, make the same choices they made and behave the way they did, then I'd be able to have what they had. Even if it meant I was very different from them. After all, I kept hearing the wise advice of faking it till you make it. As it turns out, that didn't really ever work for me. Maybe it works for some people but I'd argue that it only works up until a certain point. Then you hit a glass ceiling. The glass ceiling of who you are.

I wrote about self-comparison in the chapter titled as such (page 139), but I'll make a small point about it here. It's easy to look at snippets of other people's lives and decide that they have everything you want. That's really easy to do because you're taking a snippet, a tiny portion of their experiences out of context and filling in the blanks of everything else. That leaves you to want everything they have, even if it's not accurate. You're not factoring in what they had to endure to get where they are, who they had to fight with, what they had to overcome, who they may have lost, what they struggled with and what they continue to struggle with to keep their life moving forward.

Here's an analogy to help. You're comparing their two-hour feature film to your three years of writing, two years of finding a studio to fund the production of the movie, ten weeks of shooting the film, six months of editing and a three-week global press junket. They just don't compare. The way you're measuring your life and the life of others is dramatically different but you continue to do it as much as you can. Even if it depresses, frustrates, panics or isolates you.

The next time you start comparing yourself with other people and what they currently have, I want you to do this. Firstly, see if you can imagine where they were in their lives three to five years ago. Try to imagine and paint a picture of what their lives looked like and the things they may have been struggling with. Once you've done that, you can even try ten years earlier and do the same thing.

Now that you're getting more context of who they were and where they've come from, do the same for yourself. Look at where you are now in your life. Look at what you're struggling with and what you've achieved. Then look back three to five years and look at who you were, what you were struggling with and become aware of how far you've come since that place. Then go further back to ten years and recognise the journey you've been on.

The point here is to help you realise two things.

1. The people you're looking up to are moving away from a place in their lives and towards where they want to be.
2. You too have come far in your own life. You're not exactly who you were and where you were years ago. You've travelled further down your path. You've moved forward on your journey even if it doesn't feel like it.

When you realise your own progress, it naturally becomes difficult to measure yourself against others because you realise that who you are, the experiences you've had and what you've accomplished are all different to theirs.

You realise that two hours of edited footage came from years of work. That it's difficult to measure the two things against each other. You realise that one inch isn't the same as one centimetre and they will never be.

As the wise man Dr. Seuss once wrote:

"Today you are you, that is truer than true. There is no one alive who is youer than you."

It's time to change the measuring tape that you're using to measure your life. It's time to start using the yardstick you were born with. Recognise that you haven't stood still in your life even though it may have felt that way. You've moved forward. You're not where you used to be. When you stop the self-comparison and start becoming the role model you've always been for yourself, you create more space in your life to be you. The real you. The you that you've always wanted to be. The you that you were destined to be.

Don't believe me? Try it for a year and look back on where you were and who you were. I bet you'll come to find someone fascinating at the other end. You'll realise that you are exactly what you've been looking for. This truth changed my life.

"If you cannot manage your emotions, you cannot manage your money."

WARREN BUFFET

USE MONEY WISELY TO CREATE WEALTH

Money – the tool used to communicate in an economy. Money fascinates me (amongst many other things, in case you haven't worked that out). Money is something that has developed a stigma, a personality, a perceived value and a power. Yet it does not inherently carry any of those things. All of these things are endowed by its master – you. Everyone operating in the economy obeys and follows the rules of how money is used – for the most part. Yet so few believe it's an entity to be tamed. It's become something of a wild horse that only a few whisperers can lure into their control. So let's blow the smoke and mirrors away with money. The way you think about money influences the way you use it.

It's a tool. It serves no other function than to be used in some way. Another way to put it is that money is an employee in your business of life. It has a job and that job is meant to be fulfilled. To treat money in any other way is what leads most people into the money traps they usually snare themselves in.

When agriculture and farming were used to harvest more food than a single household could consume, the farmers would take their excess harvest and trade it with other farmers for their goods. Wheat farmers would trade a bag of grain for two dozen eggs. The goat farmer would trade two litres of cow's milk for green vegetables. Produce was used as the tool. Then state authorities came in and instituted money as a form of exchange. Everyone agreed on the value and began to use money (something everyone would accept) as a way to trade. Makes sense, doesn't it?

Then the human ego managed to identify and associate certain characteristics with money that developed it into a cultural phenomenon that has had the same perception across the world over hundreds and thousands of years.

So how to use something like money to help you get through life? Well, let's think of it as an employee. It comes into your life because you've worked for it. You've done something of service for someone. Whether it's a business or a customer, you've provided a service to someone and they've repaid you in money as opposed to returning a favour.

What you do with that earned income is what we're here to talk about. Let's look at your financial house like a traditional bank. Someone deposits money (you get paid for service) and then you've got to account for it and decide where it goes. Are you going to save that money, lend it out to others to be repaid to you with interest (invest), spend it on depreciable items (supplies) or buy yourself that bottle of wine you've been eyeing out at the vintage cellar down the road?

If you're someone who falls into the statistics then, you're probably not saving what comes in and you're even less likely to be investing the money that comes through your house. Doing neither of those things is dangerous to your future.

Think of farmers. They're not just planting seeds and harvesting crops. They're planting seeds, maintaining the crops, ensuring they're positioned to get the best yield possible and then taking some of their harvests to turn into seeds for future crops. They're building up a pipeline of crops long before dropping any seeds into the ground. Wise, isn't it? The next time you pierce your salad with your fork, remember you're eating that because someone wise was saving for the future.

Your dollars can do the same for you if you give them a chance. But if all you're doing is buying seeds, planting them and then selling the crops, what are you left with? Some profit to buy the next round of seeds. That's not sustainable and if you have a bad crop, you're left with nothing. A patch of dirt that will eventually be overrun with weeds.

Saving a portion of your income can be the difference between the anxiety of not knowing where the next dollar comes from and being able to sit down with that book you've been looking forward to reading and getting through it without a single distracting thought about that next dollar. Forget about being a multi-millionaire or global phenomenon for a moment. Let's just talk about living a life doing more of what you love without the ongoing fear of financial scarcity. Without the anxiety of an unexpected bill and the angst of having tuna salad because tinned tuna is the only thing you can justify spending your few dollars on.

You worked for your money. Are you going to put it to work for you now or let it disappear into forgettable materialism?

Snowballs are interesting metaphors to use for momentum. Like most things they start out small, and as they grow they build momentum and start to develop and exert their own force. But what you're not paying attention to is that the small amount of snow that started the ball off took some effort to build. Then after a slow start, it started to collect more of the same stuff to grow. More and more snow would stick to the ball and add to its mass. The mass would expand simply by the nature of attracting more of its own kind – snow. As the snowball makes its way down the slope, it comes into contact with more snow which sticks to the growing ball.

Money does the same. Because money, like a lot of things here, is energy. The more energy that is built, the more of the same energy that is drawn in. It's a replication of resonance. If you play a string on a guitar close enough to another guitar, the same string on a nearby guitar starts to vibrate and generate sound without having been plucked itself. That's resonance.

The same is true for money. The accumulation of money resonates and accumulates more money for a variety of reasons. One of which is that it becomes a conscious effort in your mind. You accumulate money with a meaningful intention behind it and you start to see more and more scenarios for you to accumulate more money. Doing so with meaningful intention underlying your actions makes building a snowball more of the game it was meant to be all along.

You've been playing a different game if you're anything like the statistics suggest. You're probably throwing snowballs all over the place after building a stash of them. But because you're so quick to throw them all, you quickly realise that you're left with nothing. When in the middle of a snowball fight, you're the one desperately clamouring to make a snowball while others have their own stash ready to draw from.

What if you had built a stash of snowballs and when it came to the fight you were also making them in real-time? What if you were making them and throwing the fresh ones you made while you left your stash alone? What does that make the stash? A back-up plan. That way if you can't make snowballs fast enough to keep up with the onslaught, you can lean on your back-up for help.

So the next time you go to spend your money, make sure that you're aware of what you're spending it on. Are you putting your personal employees to work? Or are you telling them to go for an aimless walk, not bothering to come back?

You're probably taking your ability to earn an income for granted. You're seeing that you are fine now. You may be earning money working a job or career and things may be okay for you. Perhaps it's going great for you. They won't always be great though. I promise you they won't. No individual, civilisation, culture, empire or economy has gone without its downfall, its winter or drought. The ones that survived, did so by preparing in advance for the inevitable downturn. They kept a certain number of seeds from their crops to make sure they had enough for future crops, even if the future crops didn't produce a harvest. They created their own insurance policies.

This may all seem pessimistic to you. Fairly so. But let me assure you that you'll refer to this chapter when things inevitably get tough and tight. You'll either be coming back here to look for what to do and how to handle what you're going through, or to thank yourself for taking action while you had the opportunity to prepare yourself. I have personally benefitted from putting seeds aside from the harvest. The emotional and mental profit far outweighs the dollar value.

Here's one more question for you in regard to your generous spending habits.

What are you investing in? Is it an important function? A way to get you further along in your life? Or are you just investing in the fleeting feeling of pleasure as an attempt to fill the void of being lost and purposeless in life?

Finding purpose to your life self-regulates the sense of fulfilment you're trying to obtain through spending. It gives a purpose to your money that is bigger than you and your fleeting feelings.

You're worth more than any money you can bring into your life. It's just a reflection of how purposeful, meaningful and valuable you see yourself as being. It's a reflection, not a determinant. Understand this and you'll stop being a servant to your money. So, moving forward, what will you do with your money, master?

"When you have to make a choice and don't make it, that is in itself a choice."

WILLIAM JAMES

MAKE BIG, OVERWHELMING DECISIONS WITH CERTAINTY

Should I? Shouldn't I? Does it make sense to go with option A or is option B the wiser choice in the long term? What happens if I go with this option and then in two months I find out that a better opportunity shows up? Am I going to be able to deal with the consequences of the decision if it was the wrong choice? What if I change my mind, can I go back on my decision?

Sound familiar? Our friend *doubt* has a wicked way of showing its ugly face at the most inconvenient times. Usually when it's most critical to move forward without the doubt. You probably experience the overwhelming burden of decision-making with a variety of life choices on a sliding scale from groceries through to where the next holiday will be. Interestingly, the word *decide* is made up of two parts. The prefix, *de-*, which means *away from* or *off*, and the suffix, *-cide*, which means kill. Meaning to *kill* off or as I like to think of it, bring death to an option.

I've written about indecision in relation to a variety of choices in life – see the chapter on learning from mistakes (page 81). This particular chapter is focussed on the bigger decisions in life. Buying a car, purchasing a home, picking a job, choosing a career, starting a business, starting a family, moving on from a family, ending a relationship, moving overseas, going on a twelve-month expedition, etc. Things that involve larger commitments. Whatever the decision is, as long as it's a big, life-altering one, then you're reading the appropriate words.

In some cases, making these choices can be a no-brainer. You see an opportunity and you go for it. Done. Decision made, life changed. Simple.

Other times it's not so simple. There are many options to factor in and all options involve your availability. Whether it's because your budget allows for it or you're not particularly attached to how things work out. The basis for your struggle is on both ends of the spectrum. You're in a situation where limitations don't get you the options you want, or the options are endless and you don't know how to refine it down to what's most valuable to you.

Both scenarios can lead you to be greeted by doubt's sibling, analysis paralysis. These two work so well together that they're able to stop the most adept individuals from moving forward. Why? Through an assault of never-ending questions (see the first paragraph).

So there you are, faced with a decision that is going to have a huge impact on your life. You've got options and you don't know which option to take. How do you filter out all of the possible scenarios to get you further down the path you want to travel?

Well, there are books on books written about books on the topic of decision-making and how many different strategies there are to get to the bottom of it. The point here is that decision-making has troubled humans for a very long time. Personally, I believe it's because everyone has a different way of navigating decisions. So when asking other people for advice on a decision, they're rarely objective about it, and they'll usually say things to you that serve to make themselves feel better about a decision they made in their past. They're using you as a reflection of themselves whether they're aware of it or not.

I don't have the luxury of doing that here. If I was to be subjective when helping people, including you, navigate big decisions, then I'd be making the decision for you as opposed to empowering you to make the decisions for yourself.

Back to your choice. Why are you finding it so hard to make a decision? Are you concerned about making a mistake? Are you worried that you won't pick the best (most valuable) option? Are you pushing yourself way beyond your comfort zone into an area that no longer reflects who you are? Are you sitting on the border of your comfort zone and have forgotten what that feels like? Are you scared to make your decision for fear of being let down by your own expectations? Are you worried that if you take the option you know you want, it would mean letting go of the story you've been telling yourself? Does it mean letting go of a lie you believed? What is it that's making this so hard? What are you so afraid of?

Answer that question now.

Why does that scare you? Why are you concerned about that?

Answer that question.

What's the worst that could happen?

Answer that question.

What's the solution available to you if the worst thing did happen?

Great. So is it really the worst thing?

Now, reassess the choices. Does it make it easier for you to see the path you want to follow?

If still no, then I have a solution for you that a mentor of mine taught me when it comes to removing bias. Here's the magic trick you're looking for. Before we go any further, I have to give you full disclosure, you have to use your head and do some mental heavy lifting.

Let's say you're struggling to decide where you want to live next. Let's say New York City. You've got an area in mind but you're not sure if you want to make the move. On a page with four columns, write in the header of each column the following...

- Benefits of moving to New York City
- Drawbacks of moving to New York City
- Benefits of NOT moving to New York City
- Drawbacks of NOT moving to New York City

Now, your job is to write an answer to each one as you move across the page (left to right). One benefit of moving to NYC, one drawback of moving to NYC, one benefit of not moving to NYC and one drawback of not moving to NYC. And again, and again, and again. You want to do this at least thirty lines down.

The intention here is to remove your bias, reveal some hidden agendas you may have and help you be more objective about your decision. That way you're less likely to experience the sense of being let down by your expectations, having your bubble burst about how you thought things would go, and minimise the chances of you feeling like you've made a mistake after the decision has been made. I told you, it's heavy lifting mentally, but it may just save you years of your life, tens or hundreds of thousands of dollars or starting/staying in a place in your life that no longer serves you the way you want.

Making decisions, especially the larger, life-changing decisions, involves taking a risk. If you've taken a risk in the past only to see that your gains weren't realised, then you will keep yourself in analysis paralysis as a way to avoid the decision altogether. It's an emotional protection mechanism but you're not really protecting yourself.

When it comes to taking risks, consider that you won't be able to get very far in life without taking risks. Some people interpret that statement as "go all in or all out and live life to the limit." No, that's not what I'm saying. I'm suggesting that you will be required to take risks regularly to find out what lies on the other side of that risk. You can do the above exercise to help see those risks and prepare in advance, which is wise, but there are always risks that cannot be completely pre-empted. If you're scared of what might happen should those situations surface along your journey, then read the chapter on learning from your mistakes (page 81). It will also do wonders if past mistakes are driving your indecision.

Taking risks is a scary act. Even those at the top of their game whom you admire take scary risks. Theirs are just different for them than they were ten years earlier or long before anyone, including you, knew their name. The level of risk you play at will progress as you step through your life. So when it comes to making big, life-changing decisions, are you risking what you have to get more stuff? Or are you taking a risk on yourself to learn more about who you are and what you're capable of?

If your answer is yes to the first, then it might be worth reconsidering the options. If it's yes to the second one then you can't mess that up. As long as you choose to learn about yourself, you'll reap rewards. Choose your growth every time and you can't make a mistake. Now, decide. Which option will you bring an end to?

"The use of money is all the advantage there is in having money."

BENJAMIN FRANKLIN

LET GO OF SCARCITY

It's tempting to collect and accumulate in life. There's a lot of material things around us that we can easily keep. Things that come into our lives and that we hold onto. Like a beaver who's built a dam, collecting more water than it needs and trapping more fish than it needs.

There's a sense of gluttony that comes with this. A borderline greed. As if you're taking more than your fair share of what's to go around. Like a zero-sum game. The more you take, the fewer others have.

For the most part, greed seems like an overextension of power. Someone develops enough power to take, they continue to take and then it eventually turns into hoarding of sorts. Those who are perceived to be greedy tend to be perceived in such ways by those who are conflicted about receiving or taking in their own lives. Those who are being cast as greedy believe they've earned theirs and don't owe it to others.

Here's where emotions come in to help understand both sides of this same coin — pardon the money pun. Greed, as I said, appears to be an abuse of some degree of power. But in truth, what appears to be greed or gluttony is actually fear. Fear of scarcity. Worry that there won't be enough for them. So collection takes place, stockpiles are built for the winter — the downturn. They worry that the drought will come again and wreak the same havoc it did last time. They worry that the pain they experienced from the sense of scarcity will come to visit again. So they stockpile.

Contrastingly, those too noble to take and receive, who seem to be good-natured altruists, are not entirely what they seem. They live in fear too. They fear the pain of others. They fear experiencing the guilt they might have if they take from another. They fear the possibility of being judged and ostracised in their community or tribe for rising to the top of the crowd. They worry that as they flap amongst the flock, they may have wings so strong that they lead the migration unexpectedly. Or worse yet, they worry that they fly so far forward that they fly alone.

Both sides of the coin are fear based. They're based in a sense of scarcity, finite resources, a zero-sum game that leaves a loser for every winner. This belief is paradoxically what leaves everyone a loser.

On one side you have the bird who wants to fly off at a natural pace choosing to stay in the flock out of fear, and on the other side the glutton who fears poverty is collecting so much that people choose to stay away from them. Who wins in these situations? No one.

On the surface, it seems that I'm suggesting you to do neither. Don't fly off and don't collect too much. That's not what I'm suggesting. Like most things I teach, I suggest addressing the underlying motivator. The force that's driving the behaviour in the first place. The emotion, the fear. This is what's pushing otherwise centred people off-balance.

By all means, collect, build, accumulate, but do so having full awareness of what's driving or inspiring you to do so. If it's your desire to build and create things in your life that are bigger than you, things that contribute to a greater society than yourself, then go large. In cases like this, the more you earn, the more you can serve. Accumulate your wealth as it suits your vision, whatever the form your wealth needs to be. But if you're accumulating due to your own self-centred fears, then like a beaver, you end up building a dam filled with swampy, stale water with you at the centre of it. This serves no one and hardly serves yourself any more than having somewhere slimy to swim.

The same is true if you want to flap your wings and separate from the flock. If you want to rise above the common thinking of your collective group but you're too afraid to do so, who are you thinking of? Who are you focussed on? Yourself. This, like our greedy beaver, is just as self-centred. You're too afraid to move off to your own heights so you keep yourself in the pack. However, how much are you serving the pack by keeping yourself there begrudgingly? You become a weight or a burden to the collective group and forfeit the opportunity to be of greater service to people outside of your pack who are waiting for someone like you to show them what's possible.

There's a balance for you to strike between these two. You don't have to let fear and scarcity keep you hostage.

The only one holding you captive to these ideas is you. Especially now that you've read these words. The sense of scarcity you believe in was once warranted, but you see and think differently now. You have a knowledge that sets you free from those redundant beliefs. You have the potential to be of service to a greater collective group, a global society if you choose. Letting your fear or an unfounded sense of scarcity lead you to sabotage your service and your contribution would mean that everyone loses.

You're more than your fears. So much more. It's time to break the dam wall and separate yourself from the flock. Share what you have to offer and accept what you're worthy of. That makes everyone a winner, including you. The water will then run fresh and a flock will come fly with you.

“Wisdom is not wisdom when it is derived from books alone.”

HORACE

CONCLUSION

You will be tempted to intellectualise what you've read in this book. Meaning, you will find ways to understand what you've learnt.

Understanding and appreciation are separated by a small line. That line is the difference between integrating what you've learnt and not.

Integrate means 'make whole' in Latin.

Information and knowledge are only a 'part' of the learning process. Experience is another 'part'. Application or integration is uniting this knowledge with your experience to make the learning whole.

How do you know that something is integrated versus intellectualised? Simple. Once something has been integrated into your life and your mind, you can't unsee it. When you take an insight and apply it to your experience, you've now developed a new perspective which is different to your old perspective. You know you've integrated what you've learnt because you will struggle to get yourself back to your old perspective. You may find that it requires a large degree of mental force to even imagine what it felt like to be in the same mindset about the issue that you used to be in.

The integration of what you've learnt in these pages will happen progressively and in its own natural way. This is why it's wise to keep in mind the difference between understanding something and appreciating it.

Remember to be lenient with your past self. The judgments you have of yourself and of others before reading this book are unwarranted. You didn't know any different from what you knew at the time. The same is true for now. Except that you've now been catapulted into a new paradigm of thinking and perceiving.

So long as you are doing what you can with what you have, you will get to the end of your life having known that you gave this experience everything you had. That is enough. It always has been. Because you are enough.

Love yourself for every stage of your evolution through your life, including this one as you transition into a new level of consciousness. Everything you've experienced has prepared you for this moment and for what comes next. That is always true at every moment.

Now, step forward with your compass. You have a journey to resume.

ACKNOWLEDGMENTS

First and foremost, a special thank you goes to my parents. Without the childhood, upbringing and environment you both created for me, I wouldn't be the person I am today with the deep intrigue and curiosity of the mind and life that I have. Thank you for that gift.

To my many teachers and mentors over the years, both in death and life, you've all gifted me with a deep vault of knowledge and wisdom that would've taken me a lifetime to discover. A special thanks to Dr. John Demartini for your dedication to bringing the vast world of many fields together for me to develop a deeper understanding of life. And your insistence on making sure the message sinks in.

To all of my clients and students of past, present and future, you've continually reminded me of why I was called down this path. I consider myself privileged and honoured to have been of service to you. Thank you for believing in what I have learned. I stay the course for you.

A thank you to Emily Gowor for helping make sure this book came into print and into the hands of readers. It wouldn't be the book it is without your help.

To my wife, Diane, for being patient with me as I've thrown myself at my studies, my work and this book. Your care and attention for the recipients of this work is what has gotten me through the various challenges, obstacles and growth this endeavour has had in store for me.

Lastly, to you, the reader. Thank you for choosing to read this book. I don't call it my book because it's not mine. It's yours. The only reason I'd be considered an author is because you've read a book that I've had the honour of writing. You were in my mind as I wrote every page and paragraph. You kept me writing when I thought there was no more to write. Thank you for inspiring and drawing these writings out of my mind.

This book is for you.

ABOUT THE AUTHOR

Giorgio Genaus is a teacher, writer and mindset coach for leaders looking to deepen their sense of meaning and fulfilment in life.

After wrestling with many health and life challenges, he discovered the world of the mind-body connection. Learning about the connection between perceived stresses and the body's physiological response to stress expanded his explorations into human behaviour and psychology. These fields revealed the influence our perceptions have on the decisions we make and how we live our lives.

Now, with over a decade of experience, Giorgio has had the opportunity to privately consult a wide variety of clients including CEO's & Executives of multimillion-dollar companies, Mindset and Business Coaches, Nurses, Doctors, Counsellors, Public Speakers, Air Force Pilots, Lawyers, Filmmakers, Musicians, Record Producers, Authors and Writers alike.

With a focus on mindset, human behaviour and philosophy, Giorgio continues to share his learnings with clients through his group coaching programs and workshops.

To find out more about Giorgio and his growing body of work, visit: www.giorgiogenaus.com

www.ingramcontent.com/pod-product-compliance
Ingram Content Group UK Ltd.
Pitfield, Milton Keynes, MK11 3LW, UK
UKHW040150310726
14061UKWH00006BB/200/J

9 780645 196900